Updating Kitchens & Baths

Mark Johanson

Handyman Club Library™

Handyman Club of America
Minneapolis, Minnesota

Updating Kitchens & Baths

By Mark Johanson

CREDITS

Mike Vail
*Vice President, New Product &
Business Development*

Tom Carpenter
Director of Books & New Media Development

Mark Johanson
Author and Book Products Development Manager

Dan Cary
Photo Production Coordinator

Chris Marshall
Editorial Coordinator

Steve Anderson
Senior Editorial Assistant

Bill Nelson
Series Design, Art Direction and Production

Mark Macemon
Lead Photographer

Ralph Karlen
Photography

Craig Claeys, Mario Ferro
Illustrators

Dan Kennedy
Book Production Manager

**John Nadeau
Scott Andersen
Brad Classen**
Production Assistance

Michael Neaton
Design Consultant

PHOTO CREDITS
Pages 9, 12, 13, 21, 54, 75, 83, 103, 152
Avonite
Pages 141, 154
Broan Mfg. Co. Inc.
Page 81
Canac Kitchens, Ltd.
Page 115
Design House Inc.
Pages 14, 15, 75, 81, 103, 115
DuPont
Page 137
Eljer Plumbingware, Inc.
Pages 11, 14
Florida Tile Industries, Inc.
Pages 9, 13, 81, 154
Formica Corporation
Pages 7, 9, 10, 115
Kohler Co.
Pages 8, 11, 15, 16, 17, 54, 55, 146, 154
KraftMaid Cabinetry, Inc.
Pages 16, 55, 115
Maytag Appliances
Page 7
Peerless Faucet Company
Pages 11, 12, 17
Pittsburgh Corning Corporation
Pages 10, 15, 16, 151
Whirlpool Corporation
Pages 6, 74
Wilsonart International, Inc.

ISBN 1-58159-043-1

2 3 4 5 6/03 02 01 00

Handyman Club of America
12301 Whitewater Drive
Minnetonka, Minnesota 55343

www.handymanclub.com

Updating Kitchens & Baths

Table of Contents

Introduction

If you've ever taken the time to leaf through some kitchen and bathroom design catalogs or visit a design showroom, you've seen some amazing rooms. State of the art appliances, elaborate kitchen islands, huge banks of gleaming custom cabinets and countertops, inviting whirlpools and expansive vanity tops with a separate sink for everyone in the family. And you've probably thought to yourself "That would be nice... if only I had $50,000 to spend and a thousand square feet of extra floorspace to play with." The fact is, most of the kitchens and bathrooms we see and dream about just aren't destined to ever find a way into our homes. The average kitchen is less than 250 square feet, and the typical 5 ft. by 9 ft. bathroom is perfectly functional, but isn't ever going to become a glorious master bath and spa where we can retreat from the stress of everyday living. But these limitations shouldn't prevent us from working to transform our own modest kitchens and baths into efficient, pleasant and even impressive living spaces that meet our needs and satisfy our longings for a nice place to live.

A successful kitchen or bathroom remodeling project doesn't need to involve gutting the room down to bare studs and rebuilding it in a whole new image with the latest surface treatments and the newest bells and whistles. A few simple, and inexpensive, updates can make a dramatic improvement to any room. The trick is to choose the updates carefully, and to perform the work using materials that make sense for your budget and for your home.

In *Updating Kitchens & Baths* you'll find plenty of beautiful photographs of well-designed and very stylish rooms. Some of them are probably beyond most of our means, others are more achievable. In showing these photographs, our point is not to say "Your kitchen or bathroom should look like this," and we aren't promising that it will. Our purpose is to point out WHY each room is successful, and to help you look for ways you can apply a few of these success stories to your own home. When might a kitchen island make sense, and when is it a poor investment of money and space? Should you take on the expense of a custom-tiled shower and bath surround, or are there cheaper alternatives that will be just as gratifying? You won't find a lot of fancy designer talk about "work triangles" and color wheels and "U-shaped configurations." And then we show you with clear instructions and step-by-step photographs exactly how to go about performing each of the many small undertakings that make up a larger remodeling project.

A central theme is the cornerstone of the visual side of design. The checkerboard pattern of the vinyl tile, the brushed metal surfaces and the monolithic custom countertop all contribute to the general commercial feeling evoked in the kitchen to the left. The solid tone laminates covering the lower cabinets contrast effectively with the more traditional upper cabinets. Featuring a contemporary take on a typical Arts-and-Crafts knockout pattern, the upper cabinets also add just a touch of period feeling to the otherwise fully integrated combination of surfaces.

Gallery of Design Ideas

There's no real mystery to good design, at least not as far as kitchens and bathrooms go. On a very basic level, these are two rooms of many in a house. Like the others, they have specific functions we would like them to perform. Whether your remodeling project consists of only a couple of quick updates, or a complete kitchen or bathroom overhaul, making sure the room can perform its designated functions efficiently should be the number one design priority.

When laying out a kitchen, the standard approach is to try and locate the areas you use most near one another. This certainly makes sense, if your room will support it. But don't let it be an impediment to creating the kitchen you really want. If the refrigerator just wants to go at the end of the room near the pantry, let it go. And the same goes for the oven and stovetop (in fact, some designers prefer to locate the cooktop as far from the traffic areas as they can, reducing the chance of accidents).

Bathroom design tends to be dictated by the location of your plumbing. If you can accomplish what you want to make happen in your bathroom remodel without moving drain or supply pipes, by all means do it. But most larger-scale bathroom remodeling projects involve some renovation of the plumbing. Bathrooms are used differently today than they may have been used when your house was built, and the old layout may not make sense for your new fixtures. If you decide to rearrange the plumbing to allow for a double-basin sink or perhaps to add a separate shower stall (an improvement you'll really appreciate!), make sure you know exactly how big the new fixtures are, how far apart they need to be, and whether or not your plumbing system and the structure of your house will support the change. It will be well worth the cost to consult a designer or an engineer to answer these questions before you begin demolition.

Beyond the basic issues of function and layout (and

(Above) Unexpected textures and surfaces can make a bold design statement. The exposed brick wall and wood strip flooring aren't typical for a bathroom, but when combined with a well-placed chest of drawers they create warmth and interest that could not be achieved with more traditional surface treatments. Installing a pair of pedestal sinks is an effective way to introduce the convenience of two lavatories without sacrificing valuable space to a double-bowl vanity and cabinet.

(Right) A bathroom presents many opportunities for some design risk-taking. This all-glass molded sink basin and countertop is definitely on the upper-end of the lavatory spectrum, but it does demonstrate how an unusual fixture can transform a room and make it memorable.

these are complex subjects you should discuss with an expert) the rest is really mostly a matter of taste and budget. Think creatively when you plan, and don't overlook the more inexpensive building materials right off the bat. When installed correctly and with a bit of flair, even the most mundane products can be fun and expressive. Paint, for example, is one of the most frequently overlooked kitchen and bath products, but it has the power to completely change the look and the feeling of the room at a very reasonable price.

Cabinetry can have a major impact on the appearance of a room, as well as how well it functions. The sleek European cabinets in the photo to the left feature a consistent tone and style that is applied in several areas: as bases, uppers, floor-to-ceiling bookcase, and even as a base for a small island-type work area abutting the breakfast bar.

If you have the space, create a distinct dressing room adjacent to your master bath. In the photo above, the wall of an adjoining bedroom was removed to link this very masculine men's dressing room to the bathroom. Separating the bathroom (or bathroom suite) into dedicated areas is a good way to add enjoyment, or at least relaxation, to activities such as dressing and bathing.

Elements of kitchen and bathroom design can be carried over to other areas in your house. Here, kitchen cabinets are the foundation for a basement bar/entertainment area. The combination of dark-painted cabinets and glass multi-lite door panels create a rich, formal look.

A corner shower stall makes highly efficient use of valuable floor space in smaller bathrooms (and most bathrooms do fall into the "smaller" classification). The shower unit shown here has a base fashioned from the same solid surfacing material used to make the bathtub apron. Repeating materials in a few key spots of the room goes a long way toward tying a room design together.

Distinctive shapes add great interest to a kitchen or bathroom, as demonstrated by the graceful, custom-made countertop shown here. But unless you have either a lot of experience or a lot of time, you'll probably be glad you stuck to right angles by the time you're finished with your remodeling project.

Contrasting textures can be used to create a little dynamic tension in the room. Here, inlaid berber carpet adds just a touch of warmth to the hard, cold tile and glass surfaces surrounding it. By adding an exercise area at the far end, the owner of this bathroom transformed it into a multi-purpose "health spa" in the home. Think carefully about privacy needs, though, before you layer too many purposes onto any room.

(Above) Warm colors and a wood floor cause this kitchen to positively glow with inviting light. Undercabinet lights and an infusion of natural sunlight contribute to the effect. The layout of the kitchen demonstrates how an L-shaped cabinet arrangement creates a functional pocket that is a perfect location for an island cabinet, provided there is enough open space away from the cabinets. Adding small appliance receptacles is a very handy idea, but in most areas today the receptacle seen here should be GFCI-protected.

(Right) For obvious reasons, wood generally is not considered an ideal surface for wet areas like bathrooms, but the tight seams and tough finish made possible by today's prefinished wood laminate flooring systems offer a higher level of protection. The striking black color of the bathroom fixtures shows what can be achieved if you're willing to broaden the color spectrum beyond white and bone.

Older homes are seldom square, and the creative use of angles in this bathroom highlights the charm that a non-square room can provide. The angular lines of the crown molding on the cabinets and the stepped-back, split level vanity cabinet accentuate the gentle slope of the knee wall. An old-style claw foot tub adds still more nostalgia to the room.

(Above) Glass block is a perfect building material for privacy panels in bathrooms. It creates the separation you need, but because it allows light through it won't make the room feel like a series of dark cubbies. And a few well-placed pieces of greenery will help soften the hard appearance of the blocks.

(Right) This luxurious master bathroom suite has a distinct Mediterranean flavor. The archway into the shower room and the extensive use of marble tile are chiefly responsible for the design statement the bathroom makes.

(Above) As the dining room has disappeared from new house designs, the kitchen has become the primary eating area in many homes. Rather than tucking a booth or table into a dark corner, the designer of this kitchen placed a spacious dining island in the center of the room. The creative glass block base is attention-grabbing and friendly. The stylized bar stools enhance the ultra-modern effect.

(Left) Upper cabinets make terrific island bases, especially in a unit like the one shown here which has a two-level countertop. The 30-in. high glass-panel upper cabinets that support the breakfast bar overhang offer bonus storage. The lowered height creates a separation between the eating area and the food preparation area, giving the island greater intimacy for dining and a slightly formal appearance.

Good ventilation near the stove helps reduce kitchen maintenance. In island situations, you have a choice of installing a downdraft ventilation system, or running ductwork for a ceiling mounted vent like the one above, which also functions as a room divider. Soffits were used to conceal the ductwork.

Recessing a cooktop or sink in your island countertop accomplishes several important objectives. It frees up counter space and wall space, which in turn allows you more flexibility in those areas (the window on the left side of the kitchen was made possible by the removal of the stove and cooktop). Also, the location of the new cooktop is just a step or two from the sink, which reduces time spent walking back and forth between work areas.

Even a lowly backsplash can become a focal point of your kitchen. Extending from the countertop to the bottoms of the wall cabinets, the backsplash shown here is made from plastic laminate that matches the countertop. In addition to creating a formidable barrier to water, the oversized backsplash gives extra punch to the countertop color.

Solid surface countertops aren't just for kitchens. This heavy-duty vanity cabinet topper features an undermount sink molded directly to the countertop to eliminate seams where water can collect. The integral backsplash also presents a formidable barrier to water. The solid surface cabinet side has no real practical function, but contributes to the overall feeling of mass.

Corners hold many possibilities in a bathroom layout. Some hot tubs are designed specially for corner installations, making very efficient use of the floorspace. The custom tile floor, walls and tub apron are cool in the summers and very hygienic.

Mirrored wall panels can open up a tight corner, transforming it from dreary to bright and seemingly spacious. The effect is especially impressive in situations where three or more planes meet.

Appliances can be more than just useful features of your kitchen or bath. They also can be focal points of the decor. Black or dark-colored appliances tend to add richness to the room, while lighter colors bring brightness into the design.

(Left) Ease of access is a very important feature for kitchens and baths, especially if someone in your household has limited mobility. The worksurfaces and the oven in this kitchen can be reached easily from a seated position.

(Right) Custom cabinets offer an almost unlimited variety of wood types and finishes. The expansive cabinet banks and peninsula-shaped island base define the look and feel of this kitchen.

Galley style kitchens can be fitted with islands, too. This slender kitchen island greatly increases the available food preparation surface, while still allowing comfortable passage on either side.

(Above) Small kitchens can be efficient and charming, if not expansive showplaces. A simple "L" layout puts the sink, stove and dishwasher all within arm's reach of one another.

(Right) Natural light brightens a room like nothing else. Replacing an old or small window over the sink with a handsome new unit will have immediate payback and make washing dishes less unpleasant.

Pull-out worksurfaces add valuable horizontal space for food preparation. They also allow a chair or wheelchair to fit below, making them a good addition to a barrier-free room.

Tired of staring at the kitchen mess from an adjoining eating area? A narrow bank of cabinets between 42 and 48 inches high will hide most of the mess, while still allowing the cook to participate in the dinner conversation. A heat-resistant countertop is perfect for serving guests.

A dedicated snack area takes a surprising amount of pressure off the primary workstations in your kitchen. It also helps confine the mess that can be created by late night snacking, reducing cleanup times.

A glass block panel between the backsplash and the wall cabinets introduces light and delightful textures to an otherwise ordinary kitchen. Because glass block should not be used in structural bearing situations, be sure to contact an inspector or engineer before you start.

Projects

Floor-coverings

The floor is not the most glamorous part of any room, but it is easily one of the most important. A well-maintained floor that makes sense in its surroundings will not draw attention to itself, so much as point out the design successes around it. In addition to its visual appeal, a healthy floor is safe, comfortable and easy to keep clean.

To avoid damage during remodeling, wait as long as you can in your remodeling project to install the new floorcovering. But if you are replacing cabinets and major plumbing fixtures, you'll probably want to remove the old floorcoverings first—especially if any rerouting of plumbing is required. If the old cabinets and fixtures were installed on top of the subfloor, you'll want to repair or replace the subfloor before installing new cabinets and fixtures. Typically, floorcoverings are installed up to and around cabinets and fixtures.

Because kitchens and bathrooms are subject to ongoing exposure to moisture, the number of floorcoverings suitable for them is somewhat limited, especially in the case of bathrooms. Resilient sheet vinyl is probably the best all-around choice for bathrooms and can be effective in kitchens as well. Vinyl tiles are easy to install and very inexpensive, making them popular in kitchens and in drier bathroom areas. Ceramic tile is also a popular floorcovering for these rooms.

While hardwood flooring is seldom recommended for kitchens and baths, advances in prefinished, laminated plank flooring systems have eliminated most of the moisture and hygiene problems demonstrated by wood floors in the past. Carpet is not typically a good choice for either room, since it holds moisture and germs and is difficult to clean.

Resilient sheet vinyl is an excellent floorcovering choice, especially for bathrooms. The lack of seams and the natural water resistance of vinyl help form a nearly impenetrable protective covering for the subfloor. It is also a good floorcovering for kitchens, although the larger floor area usually requires some seaming and the style and color selection are somewhat limited compared to other floorcoverings.

Resilient floor tiles are also very popular floorcoverings for kitchens and baths, in part because a vinyl tile floor is about the easiest floor for a do-it-yourselfer to install. Although the selection can be somewhat limited, a resurgence in popularity of solid vinyl commercial tiles, like those shown above, has expanded design options with vinyl tile. Avoid installing vinyl tiles in very wet areas, such as the area near showers, toilet and bathtubs, as water will eventually work its way into the seams between tiles and cause them to curl and fail.

Painted floors

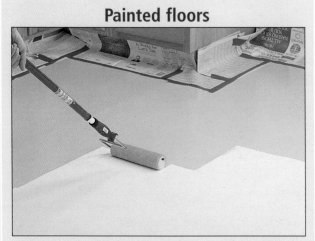

Because trends in kitchen and bathroom design change so fast, some types of floorcoverings can become painfully dated long before their useful life is over. Instead of tearing up your old sunburst linoleum, however, consider "remodeling" it with paint. Most sheet flooring and even some floor tiles will accept a painted finish that is durable and brings new life and color into your kitchen or bathroom (See pages 34 to 35).

Ceramic floor tiles add color and texture to a room and, depending on the style, can make a significant contribution to the overall design of the kitchen or bathroom. They are also extremely durable and impervious to water. But, as with tile countertops, the weak spot in ceramic tile floors is in the grout lines. If the grout lines are well-sealed and you regrout the floor periodically, you should have few, if any, problems. But even the most carefully maintained grout lines will tend to become mildewed in wet areas, and they can even present a health hazard as germs can harbor in the lines, and even on the surfaces, of some types of tile. Installation is also fairly complex and the cost is on the high side.

Removing floorcoverings

In almost all cases, plan on removing old floorcoverings before installing a new floorcovering. If the old floorcovering is thin resilient tile or sheet vinyl that's in good condition, you may be able to get away with tacking new vinyl floorcovering products directly on top of the old floorcovering. But generally, this practice is not recommended—the old floorcovering may be concealing damaged underlayment or even a moisture problem that will cause the new floorcovering to fail.

Most floorcoverings are installed over a layer of underlayment—usually ¼ in. plywood. Especially if the floorcovering has been fully bonded to the underlayment, you'll be better off removing the old underlayment along with the old floorcovering. This will let you avoid quite a bit of difficult scraping that will likely cause significant damage to the old underlayment anyway. In some cases, however, the old floorcovering may have been installed directly to the subfloor or to the surface of a hardwood floor you wish to preserve. In such cases, the best course of action is to remove the floorcovering only, then scrape away old mastic with a long-handled scraper.

In most cases, it makes more sense to remove the underlayment along with the floorcovering. Set your circular saw to cut through both layers (usually, a ½ in. cutting depth will work), then cut the floorcovering and underlayment into manageable strips and pry them away from the subfloor.

Options for removing resilient flooring & linoleum

Cut the floorcovering and underlayment into strips about 2 ft. wide, using a circular saw set to about ½ in. cutting depth (See photo, top of page). Finish the cut with a reciprocating saw or hand saw, then pull the strips away from the subfloor with a pry bar.

OPTION: If the old floorcovering was bonded to a subfloor, concrete floor or hardwood floor, slice it into strips with a utility knife and peel the strips off as best you can. Remove remaining material and adhesive with a long-handled floor scraper. Soak stubborn adhesives with warm, soapy water.

Resilient flooring includes linoleum, sheet vinyl, vinyl tile and a few other types of tile made from various composites and polymers. Most often, it is fully bonded to the floor underlayment. Whenever possible, remove the old underlayment along with the floorcovering.

NOTE: Linoleum and resilient tiles installed before the 1970s may contain asbestos and, if so, should be treated as a hazardous material. Before removing older linoleum, bring a sample to your local waste disposal authority for testing, and follow all recommendations and local regulations for removal and disposal.

Options for removing ceramic tiles

Use a cold chisel and maul to chip off old ceramic tiles. Always direct the blow away from your body and away from any floor drains, pipes or other obstructions. Use a long-handled scraper to remove old mortar if you're unable to remove the underlayment. Wear eye protection and gloves.

Chisel a pathway in ceramic tile floors to create clearance for your circular saw. Then, cut through the underlayment and remove the old floor in sections (See photo, previous page). It is possible to cut through the ceramic tile with a circular and masonry blade, but that generates a high volume of fine dust you're better off avoiding

Repairing subfloors

One of the best reasons to remove old floorcoverings and subfloors is that it gives you a chance to inspect your subfloor and floor joists for damage. With early detection, you can stave off the need to remove a perfectly good floor to attend to a problem later on when it becomes more severe. If you find rot in your subfloor, the first thing you need to do is determine the source of the moisture—usually a leaky pipe or a bad seal around a toilet, shower or bathtub. Once you have corrected the problem, repair the subfloor. If the damaged area is relatively small, cut it out with a circular saw (left photo). A circular saw set to the thickness of the subfloor is a safer tool to use than a reciprocating saw, which may cut through plumbing lines or wiring. If more than half of the subfloor sheathing sheet is damaged, simply remove the entire sheet. Try to locate cuts so they're centered over joists. Remove the bad area, inspect the joists to make sure they're not damaged, then cut a patch from exterior plywood the same thickness as the original subfloor. The patch should be about ¼ in. smaller than the opening in both directions. Secure to the floor joists with deck screws. If the floor joists are showing signs of damage or rot, contact your local building department for advice.

Choose floor underlayment material based on the type of floor covering and the general exposure to moisture. For bathroom installations, use exterior rated plywood (BC) as an underlayment, except when laying ceramic floor tile, which requires a cementboard underlayment. In drier areas, you can save a little money by using oriented strand board or lauan plywood, but only with certain types of sheet flooring.

Floor underlayment

If floor coverings are seen as lacking in glamour, floor underlayment must be truly uninspiring. But without a properly installed underlayment, even the best-quality floorcoverings can look shoddy and will be more likely to fail prematurely. For kitchens and bathrooms, building materials that can withstand exposure to moisture should be used for the underlayment. (Exceptions may be made in areas where moisture is not present, such as eat-in breakfast nooks or dressing areas in bathrooms).

Most flooring manufacturers provide specific recommendations for what material to use as an underlayment with their product. Follow these recommendations as closely as you can.

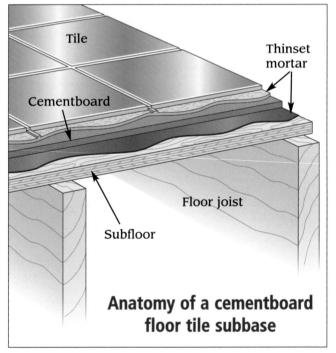

Anatomy of a cementboard floor tile subbase

Cementboard underlayment for floor tile installations is bonded to a sturdy subfloor with thinset mortar. The seams and screwheads should be taped and filled with thinset. Then, the tile can be set into a mortar bed applied over the cementboard.

The importance of smooth, clean floor underlayment

Minor irregularities may seem harmless when you're inspecting your floor underlayment, but with some types of floorcoverings (especially thinner resilient vinyl products), they will show up as glaring errors after the floorcoverings have been installed. Seams that are not taped, screw counterbores that are not filled, screw or nailheads that are not recessed and general debris can all show through your new floor, as seen in the example above.

How to install plywood flooring underlayment

Subfloor

1 Remove old underlayment entirely. Inspect the subfloor, checking for high and low spots and for rot or other types of disrepair. Cut out unsound subfloor and replace with new material (See page 23). Trowel floor leveler compound into low areas to bring the surface to level. Let the compound cure.

2 Cut and lay out all of the floor underlayment sheets before you begin attaching them to the subfloor. Start with a full 4 × 8 sheet laid in one corner. If your subfloor is also made with sheet goods, do not repeat the same sheet pattern with the underlayment. Also, use half-sheets as needed to minimize seam alignment. There should be a gap of about ⅛ in. (a 6d finish nail makes a good spacer) between sheets.

3 Attach the sheets to the subfloor with 1 in. deck screws driven at 8 in. intervals near the edges of the sheets. Also drive screws into the field area of the sheet, again at 8 in. intervals, across the entire underlayment. Screws on opposite sides of a gap should be offset slightly from one another. Drive screws so the heads are countersunk slightly.

4 If installing resilient flooring (or another thin floorcovering), mask the imperfections in the subfloor surface in much the same way you'd tape wallboard. Fill the gaps between sheets and the indentations over screws with floor leveler compound or thinset mortar, then smooth out with a trowel. If necessary, sand and feather the edges of the dried compound to create a smooth, "seamless" surface. Vacuum the floor thoroughly before installing the floorcovering and avoid walking on it.

Proving that the classics never go out of style, solid vinyl tile is making its mark once again in design circles. One of the most inexpensive floorcoverings you can buy, these tiles have a commercial look that is accentuated by the diner-style checkerboard pattern.

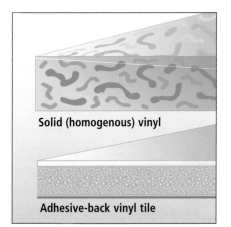

Solid (homogenous) vinyl

Adhesive-back vinyl tile

The two most common types of resilient vinyl tile you'll find in building centers are thinner, 12 × 12 in. adhesive back tiles with traditional printed patterns and 12 × 12 in. homogenous vinyl tile (like the tile in the photo above). Both types cost about the same amount per square foot.

Flooring
Resilient vinyl tile

There is probably no easier floorcovering to install than resilient vinyl tiles. The self-adhesive type, while not known for their durability or high style, can easily be slapped down in a matter of hours. Coupled with their low cost, the ease of installation has made them very popular. And for these reasons they may be the perfect floorcovering choice for your kitchen or bathroom updating project.

The category of resilient vinyl tile also includes a couple of other types of product in addition to the self-adhesive tiles (often called-

stickybacks). Thicker tiles with heavier wear layers and higher vinyl content are also relatively easy to install. Set into a bed of tile adhesive, they rank somewhat higher in durability and general quality. But you may need to go to a tile store to find them. Solid "homogenous" vinyl tiles with a commercial look are increasing in availability, even in general building centers. Manufacturers now offer them in dozens of different colors with their distinctive "linoleum swirl."

How to lay floor tile

Note: The general layout information contained in the following sequence can easily be transferred to the installation of any type of floor tile, including ceramic tile.

1 Before starting your tile installation, prepare the floor underlayment as shown on pages 24 to 25. There are many ways of going about creating a layout for a tile flooring project. One of the most common is to base the layout on the primary entryway into the room. This area receives the most traffic and is the most visible. Remove or loosen transition pieces at adjoining floor coverings, then use a straightedge to draw a reference line at the entryway, parallel to the wall.

2 Mark the midpoint of the entryway area on the reference line (for example, if the door opening is 32 in. wide, measure 16 in. from one jamb). Since most vinyl tile is 12 in. square, the best layout is normally achieved by centering the middle tile on the midpoint then trimming the end tiles in the opening to fit around the jambs. If you're installing smaller floor tiles, you may want the midpoint of the entry area to fall along a seam or grout line. For our 12 in. tiles, we measured over 6 in. from the midpoint and made a reference mark. Then we extended that reference mark out into the room with a framing square, making sure the line was perpendicular to the entryway.

First reference line

3 Establish perpendicular layout lines to divide the floor into quadrants. The first line is the extended reference line you drew in step 1. To locate the second reference line, dry-lay several tiles along the first line, starting with the first tile in the doorway (it should "underlap" the transition area). Then, trace the leading edge of the tile closest to the center of the room. With a framing square, extend this line in both directions from the first line. This will result in perpendicular lines that will fall at seam locations.

4 Begin applying tile adhesive for one quadrant of the layout. Until you're comfortable with the technique, apply adhesive for only a half-dozen tiles or so. Use a square-notched trowel to apply the adhesive (check the manufacturer's application recommendations before selecting a notched trowel). Coat the corner of the first quadrant, using a square cross-hatch pattern of alternating ridge directions. Try not to obscure the layout lines.

5 Lay one corner tile in the quadrant, pressing it into the adhesive with a twisting motion. Take care not to displace too much of the adhesive, but make sure the tile is fully seated. The tile's edges should align with the layout lines in the corner.

6 Lay the tiles on each side of the corner tile, making sure they're flush against the edge of the corner tile and aligned with the layout lines. For our layout pattern, we alternated tile colors while we oriented the grain direction the same way for all tiles. Add the next tile in each run, then begin filling in the middle area. Apply tiles over the entire area that's coated with adhesive. Wipe up any squeeze-out at seams immediately.

7 Fill out the quadrant, taking care to maintain your tiling pattern. At the end (border) area of the quadrant, you'll probably need to cut tiles. To mark vinyl tiles for cutting, first slip a ¼ in. thick spacer next to the wall (do not run tiles flush up against the wall). Tile the field area up to the last row of full tiles, then lay a full tile (no adhesive) on top of the last tile row. Lay another tile on top of this one, but butt the end up against the spacer at the wall. Trace along the end farthest from the wall to mark a cutting line on the loose tile in the middle.

8 Cut the tiles for the border row with a utility knife and straightedge cutting guide. Lay the tile on a scrap wood backer board to avoid scarring the floor. For commercial resilient tiles (like those shown here) score the tile a couple of times along the cutting line, then snap it over the edge of a worksurface or board as you would when cutting wallboard. Thinner composition tiles should be cut all the way through with a utility knife. Install the cut tiles along the border.

9 Make cardboard templates for inside and outside corners, as well as for any obstructions you must tile around. Trace the template onto a tile and cut to fit.

10 Fill in the remaining quadrants. Avoid walking on freshly laid tiles. But if you must, lay down a piece of plywood scrap to distribute your weight.

11 When you're finished, make a final inspection of the seams to make sure there are no ridges between tiles. Then, roll the entire floor surface with a floor roller (a rental item). Let the tile dry undisturbed as long as required by the adhesive manufacturer.

12 Clean up any adhesive residue with a rag lightly dampened in mineral spirits, or another solvent if directed by the adhesive manufacturer. Install base trim (we used vinyl cove base adhesive). Because the commercial tile we installed does not have a glossy wear layer, we rented a floor buffer and applied three coats of floor wax for a high, protective gloss.

A seamless blanket of vinyl makes an excellent floorcovering choice for any bathroom, and can be effective in kitchens as well. Most sheet vinyl sold at building centers is fairly neutral in color and pattern, which may not completely satisfy your design needs. But from a practical standpoint it's hard to beat.

Higher-grade

Lower-grade

Resilient sheet flooring is manufactured in several quality grades. Generally, you're better off avoiding the very thin products usually sold in precut and prepackaged rolls in favor of product with a thicker vinyl layer, usually purchased by the lineal foot from 6 or 12 ft. wide rolls.

Flooring
Resilient sheet flooring

The introduction of resilient sheet flooring has created a minor revolution in bathroom and kitchen floorcoverings in the past generation. Among the many reasons for its popularity are the water-impervious, seamless surface it creates and its exceptionally low maintenance requirement when installed correctly.

There are two basic methods for installing resilient sheet flooring: *full-bond,* where the entire sheet is glued to the floor underlayment with flooring adhesive; and *perimeter bond,* where only the border areas are bonded. For kitchens and bathroom, which tend to get quite

a bit of traffic and are constantly exposed to moisture, a full-bond installation is recommended. Some manufacturers recently have developed resilient sheet flooring that is designed to be installed without adhesive bonding so it can be replaced easily as style trends change. Although it's a new and still somewhat unestablished product, you may want to ask your flooring distributor about it.

The real trick to installing resilient sheet flooring is in the cutting. Making a full-size template of the room, then cutting the flooring to size off-site is the best way to guarantee accurate results.

How to make a floor template

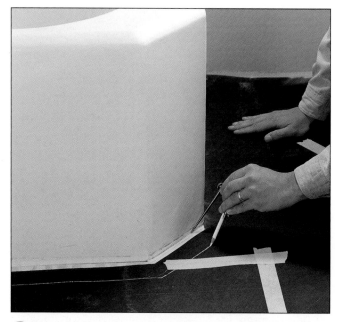

1 The surest way to guarantee a successful sheet flooring installation is to construct a full-size template of the room layout, including cutouts for obstructions like pipes and ductwork. You can use newspaper or kraft paper to make the template, but you'll get better results with 15# building paper or special-purpose template material sold by floorcovering manufacturers. Start by laying one piece of template material flat in a corner of the room, ¼ to ½ in. from each wall.

2 Tape additional pieces of template paper together in series, following the shape of the room. To keep the papers from sliding, make triangular cutouts in the paper then tape the paper to the floor through the cutouts. Fill out as much of the field area as you can. Don't skimp with the masking tape: make sure the pieces are well-secured. When you reach obstructions or corners, cut smaller pieces of template material and trace the profile of the obstruction onto the material with a compass.

3 Cut out the template sheets and tape them in correct position relative to the wall. TIP: Use a white colored pencil to draw cutting lines on building paper.

4 Continue adding template material until the room-size template is completed. When using rigid material like building paper, it's not necessary to fill in the general field area in the center of the room, but if you're using flimsier material, make an entire "quilt" that's a mirror image of the floor area. Roll the template up loosely and transport it to the site (such as a garage) where you'll be cutting the flooring.

How to cut & install sheet vinyl

1 On a clean, dry, flat surface, lay the sheet vinyl pattern-side up then fit the template (see previous page) on top of the sheet. Tape the template down to the sheet to prevent slippage. Take measurements to make sure the template is not distorted and check to make sure all of the cutout areas are the correct distance from the edges of the template. Transfer the pattern.

2 Slide the template out of the way, then cut the sheet vinyl along the cutting lines with a linoleum knife (be sure to slip a protective layer between the vinyl and the floor below). For round pipe cutouts, you can use a hole saw of the correct diameter for a clean cut. Intricate cuts can be made more easily with a pair of scissors than with a knife. Roll up the vinyl sheet.

3 Position the vinyl in the room and test the fit. Make any necessary adjustments, then fold or roll back half of the sheet. Apply flooring adhesive to the floor surface with a notched trowel, then set the vinyl into the adhesive.

4 Flip or roll the unbonded half of the sheet over the bonded half, apply adhesive to the floor, then set the second half. Be sure to get plenty of adhesive around cutouts for a good bond.

5 Roll the floor covering with a heavy floor roller (these can be rented at most building centers and rental centers), working away from the middle and toward the walls. Reinstall base shoe molding to cover gaps around perimeter.

How to make a seam in sheet vinyl

NOTE: The following information is for seaming sheet vinyl that is fully bonded to the floor.

1 Arrange the pieces to be seamed next to one another so the pattern (if any) aligns and repeats. The pieces should be exactly square to one another, with an overlap of 3 to 4 in. at the seam. Apply several pieces of heavy-duty tape (duct tape works well) across the seam to bind the pieces together. Dry-lay the sheet assembly in place and mark the location of the seam onto the floor. Remove the assembly and draw additional reference marks at the seam location. Apply flooring adhesive to the floor up to 12 in. from the seam location on one half of the area being covered by the sheets. Set the sheets into the adhesive with half of the sheet assembly folded back over the half being bonded. Then, apply adhesive to the other half of the area (to within 12 in. of the seam line) and lay the other half of the sheet assembly.

2 Roll the sheet assembly with a floor roller to set it into the adhesive. Then, lay a straightedge along the seam line and double-cut the two sheets with a utility knife held at an exact 90° angle to the floor surface.

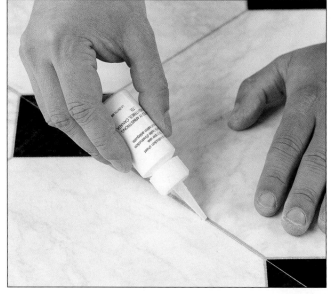

3 Fold back the edges of the sheets at the seam to expose the unbonded floor area. Apply adhesive to the area, then set the edges of the sheets into the adhesive. You may need to tug and push a little so the halves of the seam are exactly flush. Wipe up any adhesive that oozes up out of the seam, then roll each side of the seam with a floor roller or J-roller, rolling toward the seam to force any trapped air up through the gap. Let the adhesive set, then wipe the seamed area with a soft rag dipped in the solvent recommended by the manufacturer.

4 Weld the two sheets together. Nearly all sheet vinyl flooring installed in homes today is composed mostly of PVC, and can be solvent-welded in much the same way that PVC pipes are solvent-welded for plumbing. Some commercial tile can be heat-welded to close off the seam. The distributor that sold the sheet vinyl to you should also be able to provide a solvent-welding kit for seaming the flooring. The kit being used above (manufactured by Armstrong World Industries) consists of four separate chemical application steps. Follow the instructions and safety recommendations on your kit carefully.

Painting a floor may be a fairly nontraditional flooring project, but it is a great way to give a fresh, updated look to old resilient floorcoverings that are in good condition but have become outdated.

Flooring
Painting floors

These days, painted floors are found almost exclusively out of doors, usually on covered porches. But paint is also a traditional interior floor finish that simply isn't used much anymore. Concrete, wood, vinyl and linoleum are all suitable flooring materials for painting. Wood strip flooring (especially pine and fir) often was painted with solid tones, and if you're refinishing a floor of this type you may want to consider a plain painted finish. But today, paint is used in more decorative ways when applied to most floors. Contrasting borders, repeating geometric shapes and even *trompe l'oeil* images are applied to floors for an inexpensive yet highly dramatic "covering."

You can use just about any kind of paint on an interior floor, although glossy or enamel tends to be the most durable. Make sure to apply three or four coats of non-yellowing polyurethane over the painted finish for protection.

Pattern possibilities for painted floors

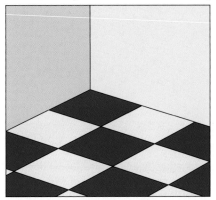

Repeating geometric patterns have a dramatic effect and are easy to paint. For best results, use masking tape to lay out the pattern, or use a painting template.

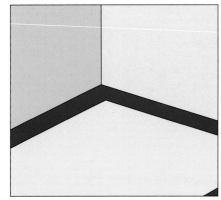

Contrasting borders add visual interest to a floor, giving the room a sense of completeness. But be aware that a painted border treatment will tend to make small rooms appear even smaller.

Trompe l'oeil is the technique of using paint to trick the eye into thinking it sees objects that aren't really there. In its simplest form, it can be used to create "faux" finishes that resemble brick pavers, genuine wood grain or even Oriental carpet patterns.

How to paint a floor

1 Thoroughly scrub the floor with hot water and detergent to remove dirt and wax build-up. If the floor has a few minor damage areas, they can be filled with latex-based floor patching compound. If your existing floor covering has more than a handful of dime-sized or bigger damaged areas, it is not a good candidate for painting. Floors with a glossy finish should be scuff-sanded with 100-grit sandpaper, then vacuumed.

2 Apply a primer that's tinted to match the same general tone as the dominant color to be used. If you're applying contrasting color, the primer should match the lightest color tone. You can use either oil-based or latex primer (if painting concrete, use masonry primer).

3 Lay out your pattern. We used masking tape to mark off an 8 in. wide border around the perimeter of the room. For borders, checkerboard and other geometric patterns, measure and draw reference lines for the masking tape.

4 We applied two coats of red paint at the border, then removed the tape, masked off the border area, and rolled two coats of moss-colored paint into the field area. Make sure to allow plenty of time for the paint to dry between coats. After all the paint has dried fully, apply three to four coats of glossy, non-yellowing polyurethane (either latex or oil-based).

Walls & wallcoverings

Walls, and wallcoverings in particular, are sometimes overlooked in the excitement of remodeling a kitchen or bathroom. When we set out to make this book for the Handyman Club of America members, we were guilty of the same oversight. Because of the many issues directly and uniquely related to kitchen and bathroom remodeling that are covered in this book, we found that there just wasn't enough space to tackle all of the complex issues surrounding walls. So we chose a few simple projects that you can accomplish whether you're dealing with all-new walls and a major remodeling project, or simply trying to make the walls you have look better.

Walls in kitchens and bathrooms require a slightly different approach than the other walls in your home because of the constant moisture they're exposed to and the fact that you'll need to clean them much more frequently. If painting, use higher gloss paint that can be wiped clean. If wallpapering, use only solid vinyl wallpaper that can withstand moisture. Ceramic wall tile is also a popular option for kitchen and bathroom wallcoverings. You'll find a useful sequence on installing tile on pages 128 to 131, where we show you how to install wall tile for a bathtub surround. It's a pretty easy step to use this information to help you create a tiled wall or backsplash.

If you need to add a little privacy to your bathroom, we've included a thorough description of how to build a stunning glass block privacy panel that will brighten any bathroom or kitchen.

Projects for updating kitchen & bathroom walls

Build a privacy wall. With today's large, multi-purpose bathroom suites, a little privacy can be a difficult thing to come by. A glass-block partition wall could be just the solution you need. Pages 46 to 51.

Install wall tile. A custom tub surround, tile wainscotting and a tile backsplash are just three of the many ways you can incorporate wall tile into your kitchen or bathroom design. Pages 128 to 131.

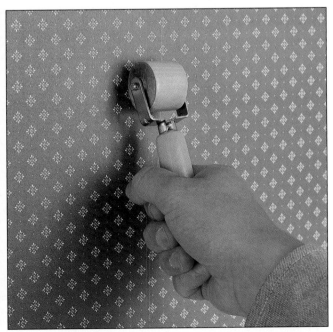

Liven up a drab wall with wallpaper. Installing vinyl, water-resistant wallpaper is a great way to bring new colors and patterns into a kitchen or bathroom. Cover whole wall surfaces, or use it for a frieze, wainscot or other accents. Pages 42 to 45.

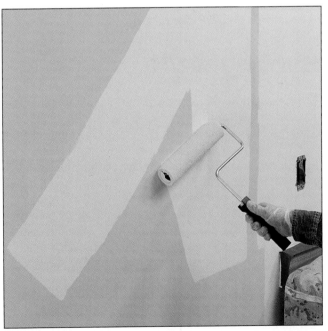

Paint and paint again. For ease of application and sheer updatability you can't beat plain old paint. Even if you've painted your house many times over, it never hurts to take a brief refresher course. Pages 38 to 41.

For a quick and easy update with immediate payback, don't underestimate the effectiveness of a fresh coat of paint. In the photos shown here, dreary and outdated harvest gold walls are given a fresh new look with ordinary white paint. White and near-white is a safe, can't-miss color for any room, but don't be afraid to take some chances with color. After all, you can always repaint if you don't like the results, and on a relative scale paint is cheap.

Painting walls

If you live in an older house with a painted kitchen or bathroom, try a little experiment: in an inconspicuous area of the room, carefully scratch the painted surface with a sharp instrument until you reach the surface of the original wallcovering. As likely as not, you'll find layer upon layer of old paint and wallpaper. In bygone days, painting the kitchen was an annual event in many households, frequently done in conjunction with spring cleaning. Owing to the closed environments, poor ventilation and accumulation of smoke and grease, it was a necessary maintenance step for purposes of simple hygiene.

Today, our attitudes about painting have changed somewhat. Improved ventilation and the development of appliances that use cleaner fuel sources have eliminated the need to paint as part of regular housekeeping, and we now see it as a purely decorative exercise. Perhaps because of this, painting a kitchen or bath has

come to be viewed as a major home decorating undertaking. In fact, it's still a relatively simple and very low-cost improvement when you do the work yourself. Even if the only issue you have with a kitchen or bathroom is that you're tired of it, that's a good enough reason to pull out the paintbrush and slap a coat or two or a cheerful new color onto the walls.

And don't be afraid to experiment a little with color or decorative effects, either. There really is no design rule anywhere that says wall color must fall within a small range of whites and off-whites, as many of us have come to believe. Pick a color that you might otherwise think of as an accent and try a splash of it on your walls. Or research and attempt a more decorative wall treatment, like sponge painting or stenciling. It may take a little getting used to, but you'll be surprised what an interesting and even inspiring room environment you can create with plain old paint.

Choosing paint

Perhaps the most difficult task in any painting project is choosing the paint. Selecting a color is a tough enough challenge by itself, but even after you've chosen the color you still will have a number of decisions to make:

Latex-based or oil-based? If you don't have good ventilation or there are children or pregnant women in your home, use latex-based paint. Otherwise, oil-based paints are preferred for kitchens because the surface is easier to clean and less likely to trap germs. For bathrooms, use latex only: it "breathes" more than oil-based and is therefore less likely to create condensation problems in moist areas. Please note, though, that with the exception of health issues, none of these are hard-and-fast rules. The best advice is to use whichever type you're most accustomed to working with.

Gloss? There is also spirited discussion among professional painters as to how much gloss is best for a painted wall in a kitchen or a bathroom. The crux of the discussion really boils down to whether you prioritize ease of clean-up or appearance. Glossier paint creates a harder, more washable surface than flat paint when dry. Obviously, in kitchens or bathrooms washability is very important. But high-gloss paints also call attention to even the smallest surface problems on your wall, which makes them unappealing to some people (See photo, right). The best compromise for most people is probably eggshell or satin.

Coverage? A typical gallon of wall paint covers 300 square feet. Especially if you're having the paint tinted at the store, buy at least 25% more than you think you'll need. Make sure you have enough for at least two coats.

Room painting sequence

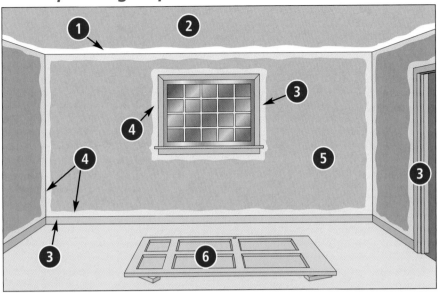

To achieve neater results and reduce the amount of "painting over" you'll need to do, divide your room up into separate project zones and paint them in a logical sequence. Start at the ceiling to avoid dripping paint on freshly painted walls. Cut in the edges of the ceiling first, then roll the field area. Next, paint woodwork and trim (use enamel trim paint). Then cut in the tops, bottoms and corners of walls before rolling the wall surfaces. Also cut in next to trim. Finally, paint doors on a level surface after removing them from their hinges.

The effects of paint sheen on observed color

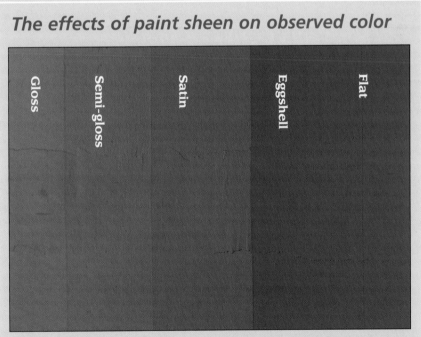

All of the sample swooshes shown above were made with the same color paint. The sheen, however, is different for each swoosh. As you can see, glossier paint reflects more light and therefore appears lighter to the eye than flatter paint. Glossier paint also emphasizes surface imperfections to a greater extent.

Tips for preparing trim for painting

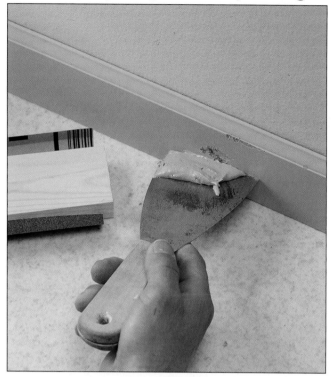

Inspect your trim, especially around windows and at baseboards, for rot or other forms of disrepair. Scrape out affected areas and fill with wood filler.

Scrape off any loose paint from trim, then fill if necessary and sand smooth so the edges are feathered out softly.

Tips for preparing walls for painting

Fill nail holes and other damage spots on walls with joint compound. A sanding sponge is an excellent tool for smoothing out filled areas prior to painting.

Protect receptacles with tape, then thoroughly wash the walls and trim you're painting with a mild solution of tri-sodium phosphate and warm water. Rinse with clean water.

Tips for painting walls & trim

Paint corners and hard-to-reach areas first, using a quality 2 to 3 in. brush (called "cutting in"). Mask the junction between walls and ceiling (unless you're painting them the same color). Take care to avoid thick accumulations of paint around the edges of the tape. The cut-in areas should be at least 2 in. wide to allow for full overlap coverage when rolling. The goal is to achieve smooth, even painted surfaces with no visible brush marks.

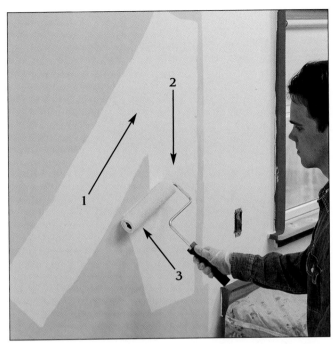

Use a paint roller to paint open areas of walls and ceilings. Don't skimp on quality when it comes to paint rollers: a good roller sleeve can cover the wall in a single coat, compared to cheaper ones that leave ridges, splotches and lint, requiring a second coat. Use a roller designed for the roughness of the wall you're painting—for most kitchens and bathrooms, a sleeve with ¼ in. nap is a good choice. When painting walls, work from top to bottom, following the rolling sequence illustrated above. At corners, try to get the end of the roller as close to the adjoining wall as possible without marring any fresh paint.

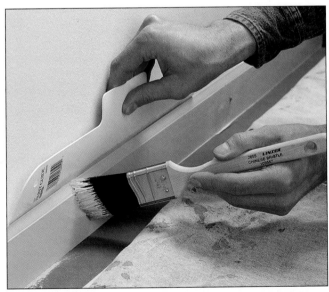

Use a paint shield or a broad taping knife to protect adjoining surfaces when painting trim. Hold the shield in place as you move the brush, then adjust the shield further down the line as you finish each section. Be sure to wipe any paint off the shield each time you move it.

Paint trim with a sash brush (a 1½ in. china bristle brush is shown here). Work paint from dry areas back in toward wet areas.

Solid vinyl, prepasted wallpaper can add new colors, textures and decorative accents to any kitchen or bathroom with a surprisingly small investment of time and effort.

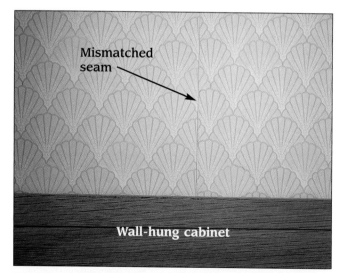

Mismatched seam

Wall-hung cabinet

TIP: Hide mismatched seams. In some wallpaper hanging projects, there will be one vertical seam on each wall where the pattern doesn't match up because one of the strips was trimmed for width. You can minimize the visual distraction by locating the mismatched seam in an area where it won't run all the way from floor to ceiling, such as above a door, window or cabinet.

Wallpapering

Applying wallpaper is seldom mentioned on most handymen's lists of favorite home improvement projects, but with today's prepasted products and their improved adhesives, wallpaper offers a chance to add character and brightness to any room with minimal effort and fuss.

Wallpaper is made from several different materials, but for kitchens and bathroom use only solid vinyl wallpaper (not just vinyl-coated). Almost all vinyl wallpaper is prepasted so, unless you're a glutton for messy work, you can successfully avoid the need to mix wallpaper paste. Prepasted wallcoverings are simply soaked for a few minutes in warm water, then unrolled and applied to the wall. There is even a brief open time with the adhesive, so you can adjust the position of each strip by sliding the strip until it is positioned just right. Before choosing a wallpaper style and color, bring a few samples home and see how they look in the actual room.

Tools and materials for applying wallpaper in a kitchen or bathroom include: water tray for immersing wallpaper roll (A); sponge for cleaning excess adhesive (B); level for establishing layout lines (C); vinyl-to-vinyl adhesive for lapping corners (D); primer for preparing wall surface (E); short-nap wallpaper brush for smoothing out wrinkles (F); plastic smoothing tool (G); wallpaper seam roller (H); utility knife with break-away blades (I); and wallpaper scissors (J).

Estimating wallpaper coverage

Calculating how much wallpaper is needed to cover your room is considerably more complicated than estimating paint coverage, but should not be intimidating. The main variable you'll need to take into account is the *pattern repeat*. The pattern repeat indicates the maximum amount two strips of wallpaper must be adjusted up or down until the pattern continues seamlessly between the two strips. Generally, the larger or more complex the pattern is, the greater the pattern repeat will be. To account for the pattern repeat when purchasing wallpaper, the safest method is simply to add the repeat length (20.87 inches on the roll shown to the right) to the height of your walls when figuring the square footage. When calculating the square footage you'll be covering, measure from the point where the wallpaper will start (either at the floor or at countertop level in most cases) and add the pattern repeat. Then multiply by the width of each wall. Do not subtract for windows or doors. Then read the wallpaper label to find the coverage amount for each roll (56 square feet in the roll shown here). Reduce this amount by 15% to allow for waste, then divide the square footage to be covered by the reduced roll coverage amount. Round up to the nearest whole number to find the number of rolls you'll need.

Read labels carefully when purchasing or ordering wallpaper. The label contains a wealth of information about the composition of the paper, suitability of use, coverage and pattern repeat. The label will also indicate pattern and which dye lot the roll is from. Make sure all your rolls are from the same dye lot.

How to apply prepasted vinyl wallpaper

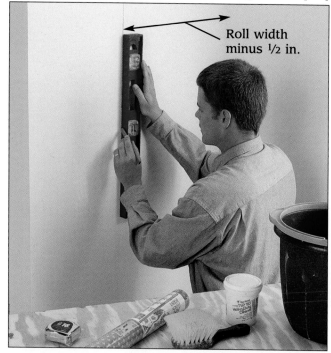

Roll width minus ½ in.

1 Prepare the wall surfaces. Scrape off all blistered or flaking paint and remove old wallpaper that's loose. Also remove textured wallpapers, even if they're in good repair. Scrub the wall with a tri-sodium phosphate and warm water solution. If the wall surfaces are uneven or cracked (for example, if you've scraped off some paint) apply a coat of wallpaper primer to the wall, following the manufacturer's application instructions. Measure out from one corner of the room and make a mark that's ½ in. closer to the corner than the full width of the wallpaper. Using a level as a guide, draw a vertical reference line through this mark. Remove wall switch plates and coverplates.

2 Cut the first wallpaper strip to length—it should be about 2 in. longer than the height of the area to be covered. TIP: Scissors are generally the best tool for cutting strips to length. Roll up the strip so the back of the paper is facing out (this helps straighten the wallpaper). The roll should be tight enough that it will fit into the water tray, but loose enough that water can circulate between folds and activate the paste. Fill the tray about halfway with warm water, then insert the rolled up strip and slosh it around to dampen all over. Check the label to see how long the manufacturer recommends immersing.

3 Carefully remove the rolled up strip from the tray using both hands. Unroll the strip on a flat, smooth surface with the pattern side facing down. Fold the ends of the strip back over so they meet midway along the strip (this is called "booking"). If the paper manufacturer suggests it, let the wallpaper sit for a few minutes to increase the adhesiveness of the paste.

4 Press the first strip in place so the edge is flush against the vertical reference line marked on the wall. The top and bottom should be overhanging slightly, and the opposite edge should overlap the corner (you'll need to cut a small slit in the top corner of the paper). Use your hands to smooth out the wallpaper strip. Take care not to disturb the strip so it falls out of alignment with the reference line. Then, use a short-nap smoothing brush to brush out any air bubbles, beginning at the top of the strip. Don't use too much force when brushing, and be sure to brush away from the center of the strip and toward the edges.

5 At the floor (baseboard) and ceiling, lay a broad putty knife at the seam and use it as a straightedge guide for trimming the wallpaper strip with a sharp utility knife. Do not trim the wallpaper at inside corners (these are generally lapped with vinyl wallpaper).

6 Before cutting the next strip, unroll the roll and position the wallpaper next to the first strip. Shift it up and down until the patterns align, then mark and cut the strip to length. Moisten and book it as with the first strip, then press it into place so the seams butt together neatly. Let the strip set up for a half hour or so, then roll the seam lightly with a wallpaper seam roller.

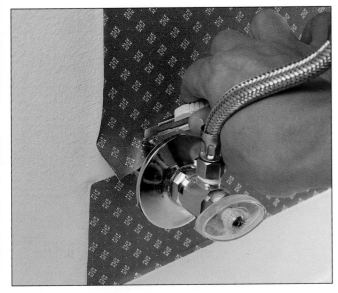

7 Fill in the rest of the wall with strips, working in sequence and taking care to match the pattern with each new strip. Cut strips to width by slicing with a sharp utility knife when the strip is booked (See step 2). Use a straightedge guide to make the cut. Cut out for obstructions such as supply pipes by cutting a slit in the wallpaper strip at the height of the obstruction, then trimming around after the paper is applied. Roll the slit with the seam roller.

8 At inside corners, overlap the first strip by about ½ in. After positioning the second strip, peel back the overlapping edge and apply a bead of vinyl-to-vinyl wallpaper adhesive to strengthen the lapped seam. Roll with a seam roller. Lay paper directly over switches and receptacles then trim around them before reattaching the cover plates. When walls are covered, wipe them with a sponge and clean water to remove adhesive residue.

Glass block privacy panel

With their open floor plans and luxurious amenities, modern bathrooms often bear a closer resemblance to a health spa than a traditional bathroom. While this emphasis on relaxation can be an enjoyable feature, it doesn't always provide the the privacy that we demand from a bathroom. A quick, easy and attractive solution to this problem is to build a small privacy panel that segments that bathroom visually.

Glass block is a versatile building material that is uniquely suited to divide a room into distinct areas without seeming to make the room smaller. It also has a clean, contemporary appearance and is relatively easy to build with. But be aware that glass block is not load bearing and should not be used as a structural building material.

Building a glass block privacy panel is similar in many ways to building a brick or block wall. The blocks are laid in rows and set in a mortar bed, with metal reinforcement used between courses. The actual products used to build with glass block look a little different than the bricks, concrete blocks and rebar you may be accustomed to working with. But the function is essentially the same. In the project shown here, we built our wall on a wood curb to protect it from impact at the busy floor level. We chose to cap the wall with two pieces of red oak that create handy ledges.

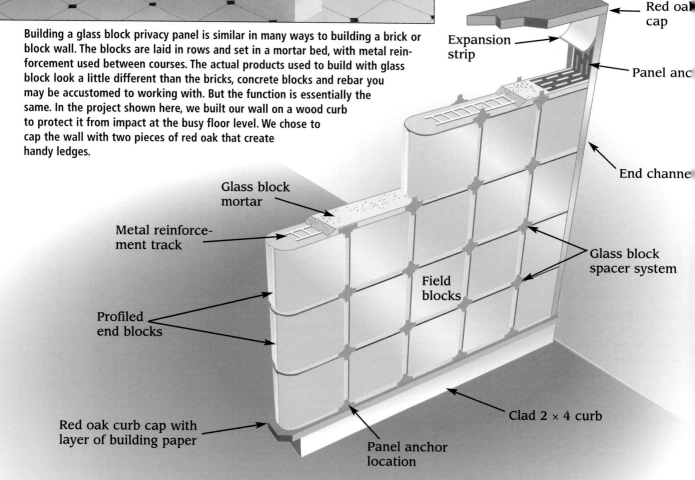

Red oak cap

Expansion strip

Panel anchor

End channel

Glass block mortar

Metal reinforcement track

Glass block spacer system

Field blocks

Profiled end blocks

Red oak curb cap with layer of building paper

Panel anchor location

Clad 2 × 4 curb

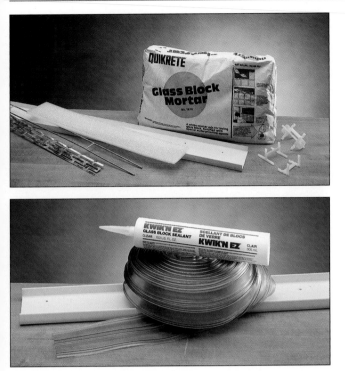

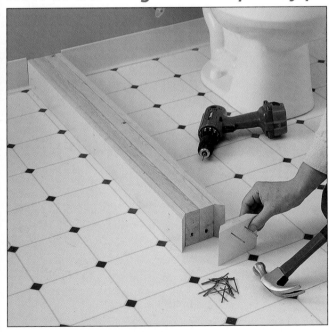

Glass block installation systems make working with glass block a simple process. The top photo shows the basic components you'll need to build a mortared block panel. The lower photo is a mortarless kit for framed panel installations made by Pittsburgh Corning.

Glass block is made in a variety of sizes and textures. Special end blocks give walls a clean, finished appearance.

How to build a glass block privacy panel

1 To protect the glass blocks from damage caused by feet, vacuum cleaners and other troublemakers, build your panel on top of a wood curb. To support the 4 in. thick blocks we used, we outlined the project area then toe-nailed 2 × 4s on-edge to the floor. Then we clad the curb with painted 1 × 4s, beveled at the ends to make bevel joints.

2 Attach a section of U-shaped end channel to the wall where it will join with the block panel. Center the channel on the curb and cut it to match the height of the wall panel. If the channel is not located at a wall framing member, drill guide holes and use toggle bolts to fasten it. NOTE: The end channel and most of the installation products used in this project, as well as the blocks themselves, were manufactured by Pittsburgh Corning. The products can be found at your building center near the glass block displays.

Panel anchor

3 Mark the location of the top of each block course on the end channel, allowing ½ in. for the mortar bed. To bond the panel to the wall, install panel anchors in the center of each mortar bed location. To prevent the panel from cracking or detaching as the wall expands and contracts, tack or glue open-cell foam expansion strips into the end channel.

4 For mostly decorative purposes, we capped the curb with a red oak board trimmed at the end to match the profiles we'd be trimming into the cap boards. TIP: If installing cap boards, cut them to size and coat them with a protective finish, like polyurethane varnish, before installing them. To protect the board and to prevent it from absorbing water from the glass block mortar, slip a layer of building paper between the board and the wall. To cut the building paper, lay a piece on the board then dry-lay the first course of blocks on top of the building paper, inserting ¼ in. spacers between the blocks. Make sure the end block is butted flush up against the end channel. Trim around the blocks with a utility knife. Then, mark the locations of the mortar joints between blocks onto the curb.

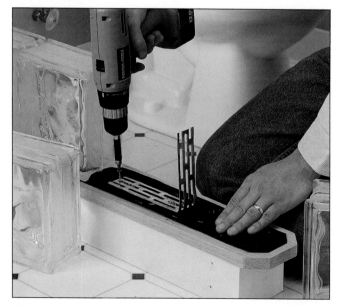

5 To help stabilize the panel, we installed an L-shaped panel anchor at the mortar joint closest to the end of the panel, using galvanized deck screws.

6 Mix glass block mortar in a bucket or mortar box, following the manufacturer's instructions. Mix no more than you can use in a half-hour. Because glass won't absorb water, the mortar should be fairly dry compared to concrete mortar. Add only enough liquid so the mortar clings together without crumbling.

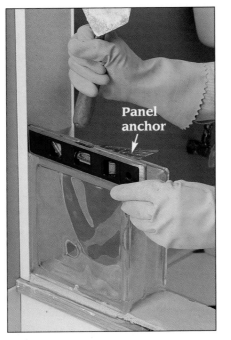

7 Lay a ½ in. thick mortar bed on the building paper layer on top of the curb. Because the scale is fairly delicate, we used a pointing trowel to apply the mortar.

8 Set the first glass block in place, butted up against the end channel. Rap lightly on the top of the block with the butt of your trowel to set it in the mortar bed. Make sure the block is level and securely seated.

9 Set a glass block spacer next to the first block, butter the vertical edge of the next block with a ¼ to ½ in. thick layer of mortar, then slip it up against the first block. Seat it with the butt of the trowel, checking with a level to make sure it's level and plumb.

Panel anchor

Glass block spacers

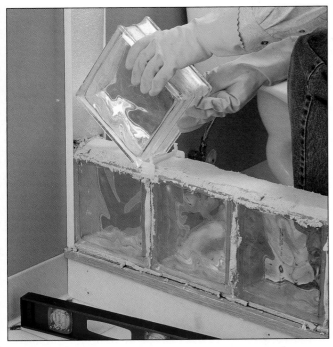

10 Lay another ½ in. thick mortar bed on top of the first course. Then, lay the second course of blocks as you laid the first. Because the privacy panel wall is not intended to bear weight, horizontal reinforcement is required only in every other course (See step 12). Lay the second course of blocks, using the glass block spacers according to the manufacturer's directions.

11 After each course (and more frequently on longer walls) pack excess mortar back into mortar joints, making sure there are no voids in any of the joints. On small panels, you should be able to postpone tooling the joints until the panel is completed, but if the mortar starts to set up, tool the joints with a mortar tool (See step 15).

12 After laying a half-thickness (¼ in.) mortar bed for the third course, add horizontal joint reinforcement to the panel. Because it is so small, the panel shown here would not necessarily have needed horizontal reinforcement, but we added it just to be on the safe side. We used light gauge metal "railroad track" style reinforcing strips made specifically for glass block walls. Press the strip down into the mortar bed and add another ¼ in. layer of mortar on top of the first.

13 Continue laying courses, reinforcing alternating rows, until you reach the top course. Because our panel is stepped, the two top courses are only three blocks long. Don't forget to check with a level periodically.

14 Lay a smooth mortar bed on the top course to help bond the blocks together and to create a flat, finished surface for the cap. Although there are several ways you can finish the top of the wall (obviously, the exposed mortar cap is not a good option), the most common method is with a decorative wood cap like we used. It's possible to set the wood cap directly into the mortar cap, but a better method is to attach it with construction adhesive after the mortar has cured (See step 17).

15 Tool the mortar joints with a mortar tool to create smooth, finished mortar lines. Tool the horizontal lines first, then tool the vertical joints, taking care not to disturb the tooled horizontal joints. Don't attempt to clean off excess mortar yet, since you're likely to mar the tooled mortar lines. Allow mortar to set for 15 minutes and then begin the clean-up. Wipe off excess mortar in a manner similar to the clean-up method for grouted ceramic tile joints (See step 13, page 102).

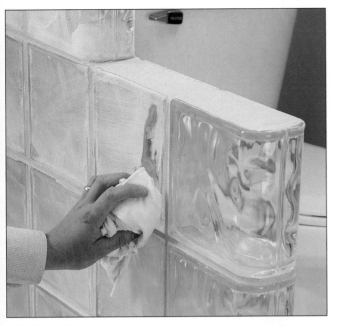

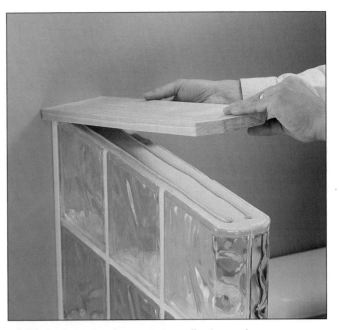

16 Let the mortar cure fully, according to the manufacturer's instructions. Brush off excess mortar from the mortar line areas with a medium-bristled brush. Then with a soft, dry cloth, buff any mortar residue off the faces of the blocks.

17 Apply beads of construction adhesive to the mortar caps and set the wood cap boards in place, pressing them down into the adhesive. If your panel is stepped, as the one shown here is, you may need to make a cutout on the lower cap to fit against the contour of the end block.

18 Apply caulk around the edges of the curb.

Cabinets

More than any other element, the cabinets make a strong statement about your kitchen, and even your bathroom. The style, the layout, the condition and their relative prominence all send a particular message to visitors to your home. Homeowners who value organization typically choose and lay out their cabinets based on efficient use of space and storage capacity. The cabinets tend to be a featured element of the room, covering every available bit of wall space and shining with the kind of glow that says either "This person takes pride in the appearance of his home" or "This person has too much time on his hands," depending on your point of view.

People who flat out love to cook tend to invest more in their appliances, which often become the feature points of the room. Cabinetry takes a back seat and often blends into the woodwork—literally. Efficient use of space and ample storage are still important, but are less important than open workspaces and good lighting.

As for the third type of kitchen owner, the socializer, cabinetry tends to be of importance only to the extent that it creates a feeling of warmth and stays out of the way well enough that several people can see each other or, better yet, sit down and enjoy a casual meal or snack together.

With these functional goals in mind, there are many ways you can update your kitchen or bathroom cabinetry without completely removing the old cabinets and replacing it with new (although in some cases this is the best plan).

Bathroom cabinetry, in most cases, is limited to a medicine cabinet and a vanity. But as bathrooms get larger (a distinct trend in new home design and home remodeling) more and more master baths include large banks of kitchen style cabinets as well.

Options for updating cabinets

Quick fixes: A thorough cleaning can go a long way toward improving the appearance of some cabinets. Painting the exterior and interior is a good option for brightening dismal cabinets. And replacing shelves or hardware also can make a big difference with relatively little investment of time.

Medium difficulty solutions: Reface cabinets and face frames with fresh veneer and replace old doors and drawer fronts. This is a great way to refresh outdated cabinets that are structurally sound.

Major projects: Remove old cabinets and replace them with new upper and lower cabinets. In addition to increasing the visual appeal of the room, installing new cabinets allows you to reconfigure your room for more efficient use of space.

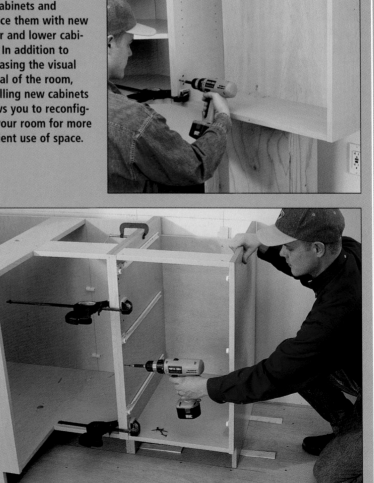

Ideas for kitchen & bathroom cabinets

Combine styles for increased interest. The solid wood panel doors on the base cabinets are contrasted nicely by the glass panel doors on the wall-hung cabinets. A shared design characteristic (here, the white face frames) gives the doors continuity.

Create built-in furniture by building with cabinets. There is no rule saying all kitchen or bathroom cabinets must fit into conventional cabinet bank layouts. In the photo above, ready-to-assemble cabinets are used to create an elegant bar at one end of a kitchen.

Cabinets are not just for kitchens. Here, a typical kitchen cabinet configuration is used effectively to create a nicely embellished bathroom vanity.

Cabinet accessories are offered by most major cabinet manufacturers. Organizers such as the pull-out pantry shown at left can help you maximize the storage capacity of your cabinets. But don't get too carried away with creating a special place for everything you plan to store: your needs may change, and someday you'll want to sell your home.

Customize your cabinets with creative colors and by surrounding them with design-rich touches, like the tartan wallpaper in this very masculine bathroom/dressing room. The green stain wash finish transforms fairly ordinary wood cabinets into a striking bank of beauty. Varying the heights of the cabinets and fitting them with a plate rail crown adds to the custom feeling.

Work with your appliances. At the very least, cabinet updates should not clash with your appliances. For a very slick appearance, you can even finish the cabinets to match your appliances or purchase matching appliance panels from the cabinet manufacturer.

Think outside the box. Renovation doesn't have to mean overhaul. Sometimes simply replacing an old cabinet (or medicine cabinet in this case) with a new and interesting cabinet is all it takes to make a dramatic change in the look and feel of a bathroom or kitchen.

Tips for cleaning cabinets

A thorough cleaning may be the only remedy your dark and dingy cabinets need to regain their original luster. To gauge the effectiveness of this remedy, try rubbing a spot on a cabinet door or drawer front with a paper towel and a mild household solvent. If the spot you wipe is noticeably cleaner than the surrounding area, plan on a comprehensive cabinet cleaning project with a wood cleaning product. For best results, remove the doors, drawers and cabinet hardware and clean them separately.

Use a wood cleaner solution to scour your cabinets clean. These products are aggressive solvents that won't cause damage to the wood finish (just to be safe, test the cleaner on a small, inconspicuous area first). Use a fine synthetic steel wool scouring pad to clean the cabinets, following the solvent manufacturer's recommendations. For added luster and protection, buff the cabinet members with two or three coats of paste wax.

Refurbish or replace cabinet hardware for a quick, dramatic improvement. Because they're the only parts of the cabinet that regularly come in direct contact with hands, knobs and pulls become dirty quickly. They're also awkward to clean when mounted and frequently they're painted over. If hardware is in good condition, scour it with household detergent (use a cotton swab or an old toothbrush to reach tighter areas). Soak painted hardware in nontoxic chemical stripper and clean with a fine steel wool pad. Rinse and repaint or coat with a protective layer of spray-on lacquer. Lubricate hinges with spray silicon or graphite. Replace screws.

Refinishing wood cabinets

Stripping off an old finish and applying a new one is a good way to restore vitality to solid wood cabinets, regardless of whether they're painted or they have a natural wood finish that is failing. Before you start, make sure the cabinets are solid wood or real wood veneer. If you don't have much experience refinishing furniture, do some research first and practice using the various solvents on scrap wood or inconspicuous areas of the cabinets. Wear protective clothing and follow the stripper manufacturer's instructions for use.

Techniques for updating cabinet interiors and shelves

Line with contact paper (top). To brighten the shelves and cabinet interior, apply durable, moisture-resistant contact paper. Clean the surfaces of the cabinet interior and shelves, then remove the backing and apply the paper according to the manufacturer's instructions. Attach shelf edge (bottom). For a decorative accent, apply hardwood shelf edge molding to the exposed edges of the cabinet shelf.

Paint the interior and shelves. Apply two coats of washable trim paint. You can paint the interior and shelves the same color as the rest of the cabinet (lighter colors tend to work better), or you can paint the interior a bright solid tone. Then, paint the shelves with an enamel accent color. Or, you can paint the interior, then apply contact paper to the shelves.

How to make new cabinet shelves

1 When possible, use the old shelves as a guide for sizing the new shelves. Otherwise, measure the width and depth of the cabinet opening and subtract ⅛ in. from the width dimension. If you're planning to tack-on shelf edge molding, subtract 1 in. from the depth dimension. If you're using veneer edge tape or simply filling and painting the shelf edge, subtract ¼ in. from the depth.

2 Cut the new shelf or shelves from ½ or ¾ in. thick plywood or melamine. Plywood has less flex than melamine-coated particleboard. Use a table saw or a circular saw with a straightedge cutting guide to cut the shelves to size.

3 Apply your edge treatment (we used ¾ in. thick shelf edge molding), then apply the finish to the shelf or shelves. Our shelves were made with oak plywood and red oak edge molding: we finished them with a coat of light stain, then two coats of polyurethane. We used a stainable wood product for the shelves because we planned to replace the old cabinet doors with new glass-panel doors. Support the shelves with shelf pins, using the existing shelf pin holes, if possible.

These dark-stained kitchen cabinets (inset photo) were dismal and dreary, but other-wise in good shape. Painting them and replacing the old hardware made a dramatic improvement in the general appearance of the kitchen.

Painting cabinets

When kitchen or bathroom cabinetry begins to show its age, your first thought might not be to grab a paintbrush. But in many situations, a fresh coating of paint is just the solution you need to effectively update your cabinetry without spending a lot of time or money.

If your old cabinets have wood or wood veneer doors, drawer fronts and face frames, they are candidates for painting. But be aware that there are some situations where paint might not be appropriate. For example, a formal kitchen with plentiful natural wood millwork and large banks of wood cabinets with valances, onlays or other wood ornamentation might not benefit from paint. Cabinetry that exhibits a particular style known for natural wood finishes (such as Arts & Crafts or Shaker) may look a little off if painted.

Use an easy-to-clean trim paint with a glossy, enamel finish to paint cabinets. A brush or roller is fine, but for best results remove the doors and drawer fronts and paint them with a good paint sprayer.

Before you commit yourself to a cabinet painting project, inspect the surfaces closely to make sure they're suitable for painting. Inexpensive cabinets often are made with plastic or foil simulated wood grain surfaces. These surfaces will not bond well with paint so you won't achieve lasting results, as you can see on the drawer front shown above.

How to paint cabinets

1 Remove drawers, doors and hardware. If you have a well-ventilated work area, plan on painting the doors and drawer fronts there. Otherwise, lay a tarp on your floor and prop the doors and drawer fronts up on wood blocks for painting. Wash all surfaces thoroughly with a TSP solution, then rinse with clean water.

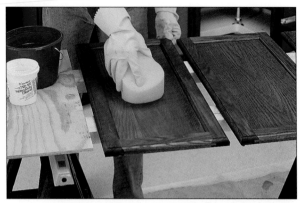

2 Fill nail or screw holes, cracks and other defects with wood filler, then sand smooth after it dries. Scrape off any loose or flaking paint or top-coating material, then feather the edges of the scraped areas with sandpaper. Apply a thin coat of primer to the cabinet sides, face frame, doors and drawer fronts.

3 Paint the face frames, starting with the inside edges. On the outer faces, paint the horizontal rails first, then paint the vertical stiles. Plan your work so any visible brush strokes follow the grain of the face frame member being painted. Paint the cabinet sides last, using a roller if access is adequate.

4 Paint the doors and drawer fronts. Use a sash brush to paint the face frames on panel-type doors, then paint the panels with a paint roller (a 5 in. roller is a good choice, although you can use a standard 9 in. roller if all the doors are larger). Paint the back sides of doors and drawer fronts—failing to paint both sides can cause warping.

5 Apply two coats of paint, then rehang doors and drawer fronts. If the hardware screw holes are stripped, drive a wood plug (the tapered end of a golf tee works well) into the hole and carefully trim off the end. Then, drill a new pilot hole.

Refacing cabinets is a less expensive alternative to replacing existing cabinetry. In refacing, the cabinet sides and face frames are covered with new veneer. Normally, the doors, drawer fronts and hardware are replaced.

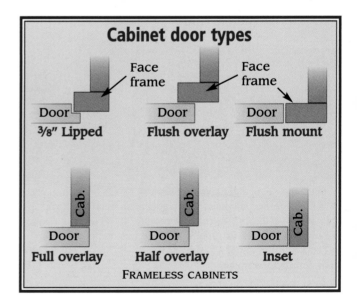

Refacing cabinets

Refacing cabinets involves applying new wood veneer to the exposed cabinet cases and face frames, and in most cases replacing the doors and drawer fronts. NOTE: If your door and drawer fronts are simple overlay types with no frames or beveled profile, you may consider refacing them with fresh veneer as well. New cabinet hardware typically is installed to complete a refacing project.

Supplies for cabinet refacing can be found at any home center. Order or obtain the doors and drawer fronts first, then purchase veneer to match. If your door and drawer fronts are made from wood other than red oak, maple or birch you'll probably need to search for matching veneer at a lumberyard.

Cabinet door types

Face frame — ³⁄₈" Lipped

Face frame — Flush overlay

Flush mount

Full overlay

Half overlay

Inset

FRAMELESS CABINETS

How to reface cabinets

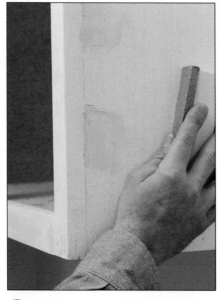

1 Measure all doors and drawer fronts, and record their sizes on a sketch of your cabinetry. Remove the doors, drawers, cabinet hardware and shelving. Number the shelves so you can reinstall them in the correct cabinets, or take measurements if making new shelves. Order new doors and drawer fronts using the old ones as sizing guides if they're the same types (See illustration, previous page).

2 Clean the cabinets thoroughly (See page 56). Fill nail and screw holes with wood putty then sand smooth. Repair other wood defects. If the cabinets are painted with glossy paint, prepare them for veneering by scuff-sanding with a power sander and 120-grit sandpaper. Wipe clean with a tack cloth.

3 Cut pieces of veneer to match the width of the cabinet ends. Before removing the backing, hold each veneer piece against the cabinet and mark it for trimming. Cut the strips to length (about ½ in. longer than the cabinet height) so they can be trimmed to fit later. Remove the backing and press in place. Trim the bottom edges with a veneer trimmer so they're flush with the cabinet bottom.

4 Cut strips of veneer ½ in. wider and longer than the face frame members, using a utility knife. Begin veneering the face frame by applying veneer strips to the end stiles: peel back the facing at one end, then adhere the veneer at the top of the stile so it overhangs both sides of the face frame. Press the veneer in place, pulling off the backing as you work toward the bottom of the stile. A piece of plexiglas with beveled edges can be used to smooth the veneer.

5 Trim the edges and ends of the veneer using a veneer trimmer or a utility knife. This will create a "tab" at the bottom of the stile. The tab will be trimmed off when double-cutting the abutting veneer strip.

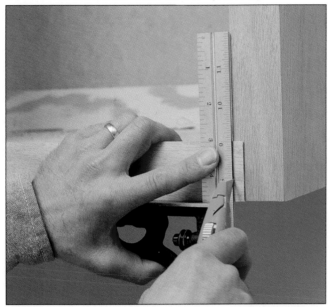

6 Apply veneer strips to the rails. At one end, press a strip against the stile veneer (use a combination square and utility knife to make a square end cut on the new strip first). Overlap the stile veneer at the other end, without removing the backing at the seam. Following a straightedge guide, "double-cut" through both the stile and rail veneer. The cut should follow the line of the inside stile edge. Remove the cut pieces, peel off the rest of the backing, then roll the veneer strips with a J-roller.

7 Sand and finish the cabinet ends and face frame. Sand to at least 150-grit, and take care not to sand through the veneer. A wipe-on stain works best, followed by 2 to 3 coats of water-based polyurethane.

8 Apply finish to the cabinet doors and drawer fronts. We used an HVLP sprayer to apply light coats of water-based polyurethane for a professional finish.

9 Drill screw guide holes for door handles and drawer pulls. A simple jig made from scrapwood can be used to ensure that hardware is in uniform position on all doors and drawer fronts. To make the jig, affix a wood strip to the outside edge of a square piece of scrapwood. Drill guide holes in the scrapwood corresponding to the correct locations for the screw guide holes on the door or drawer front. Position the jig at each corner requiring a screw guide hole and drill the screw guide holes through the guide holes in the jig.

10 Attach door hinges. Whichever hinge style you choose, it's usually easier to start by attaching the hinge to the door first. Then, use the unattached hinge leaf as a template for tracing the position of the hinge onto the cabinet when the door is properly positioned.

11 Attach the hinge assembly to the cabinet face frame next to the door opening (make sure you follow the manufacturer's instructions for hinge placement). Hang the door and adjust the hinge as needed so the door is centered properly over the door opening and the tops and bottoms of all the doors in each row are aligned.

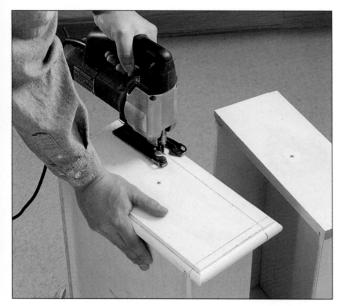

12 If your old drawers are overlay style but do not have a separate drawer front attached to the drawer box, it's usually easier to trim the edges of the existing drawer front flush with the edges of the drawer box than to remove the old front and try to join the new front to the drawer sides (these joints often are made with mortises). Use a jig saw to trim the old drawer front. NOTE: If you need to do this step, you'll also likely need to relocate the drawer slides.

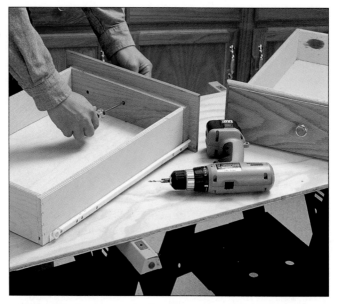

13 With the drawers in the appropriate drawer openings, center the correct drawer front over each box. Make sure the drawer fronts are aligned in each row, then poke a nail through the screw guide holes on the inside face of the front of the drawer box to mark drilling points on the new drawer front. Remove the drawer, drill guide holes, then attach the drawer fronts. Attach each knob or pull. Reinstall the drawers.

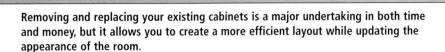

Before

Removing and replacing your existing cabinets is a major undertaking in both time and money, but it allows you to create a more efficient layout while updating the appearance of the room.

Installing new cabinets

For economy's sake, many designers view replacing old cabinets with all-new units as a last resort that's done for one of two reasons: the cabinet layout is being reconfigured or expanded; or, the old cabinets are simply not in good condition. Not only is installing new cabinets the most expensive single cost in most major kitchen remodeling projects, it is time consuming and requires plenty of demolition and disposal time. So if there is a possibility you can get by with a cheaper option, such as refacing or painting, think seriously before you start ripping out cabinets.

If you decide to go ahead and replace your old cabinets, the good news is that installing the new ones is a very manageable project for the do-it-yourselfer. And by coming up with a new layout that uses only stock

cabinet sizes, you can avoid the costs of custom and special-order cabinetry. But before you go to your local building center and fill your shopping cart with cartons of ready-to-assemble cabinets, here are a few planning tips to keep in mind:

• Take careful measurements of the kitchen or bathroom space and draw a comprehensive plan based on available stock sizes.

• Don't forget to include the prices of cabinet doors and hardware when estimating costs. These items are sold separately when you buy ready-to-assemble cabinets off the floor, and can cost more than the cabinets.

• Buy the cabinets you like best if you can possibly afford to. The cheapest cabinets in the store are still going to add up to a substantial cost, so why not spend a little bit more to get what you really want?

Upper (wall) cabinet examples

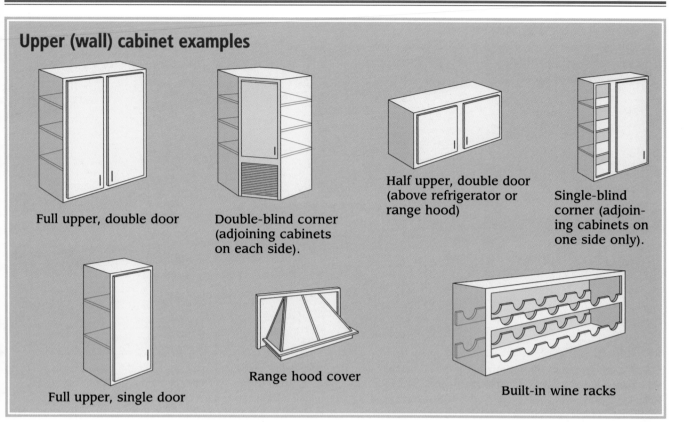

Full upper, double door

Double-blind corner (adjoining cabinets on each side).

Half upper, double door (above refrigerator or range hood)

Single-blind corner (adjoining cabinets on one side only).

Full upper, single door

Range hood cover

Built-in wine racks

Wall-hung (upper) cabinet types come in standard heights ranging from 12 to 48 in., with 30 in. being the most common height (typically stopping short of the ceiling). Width depends greatly on the style. Single-door cabinets generally come as narrow as 9 in., and double-door cabinets start at 24 in. in width. They are seldom wider than 36 in., but can be ordered as wide as 48 in.

Base cabinet examples

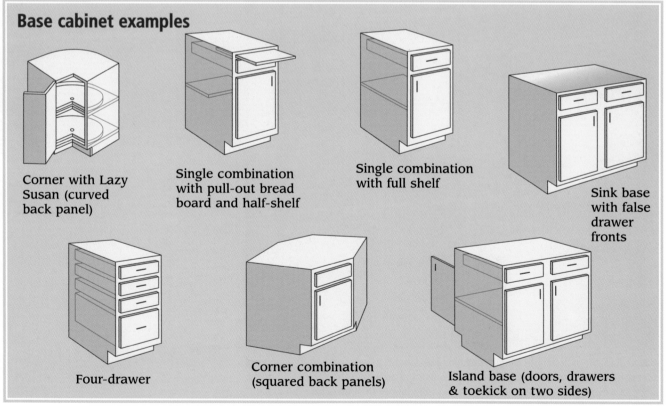

Corner with Lazy Susan (curved back panel)

Single combination with pull-out bread board and half-shelf

Single combination with full shelf

Sink base with false drawer fronts

Four-drawer

Corner combination (squared back panels)

Island base (doors, drawers & toekick on two sides)

Base cabinets come in a standard height of 34½ in. When combined with a 1½ in. thick countertop or countertop with build-up, this creates a base with a surface that's 36 in. above the floor. Configurations vary, with width generally echoing upper cabinet widths.

Buying new cabinets

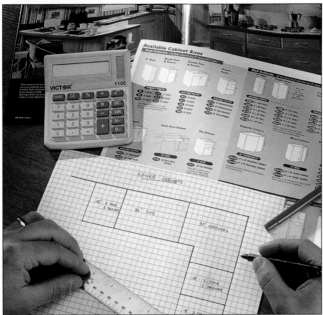

Crown molding

Filler strip

Toekick

Sketch your new cabinet layout carefully before ordering cabinets. Share your sketch with the millwork specialist at your building materials or home center. He or she may have some suggestions to help you plan a layout that meets your needs and doesn't require custom-sized cabinets.

Accessories that should be ordered at the same time as your prefinished cabinets include filler strips, toekicks and crown molding for upper cabinets. If you purchase unfinished cabinets, you may find it easier and cheaper to make these parts yourself from raw lumber of the same species.

Ready-to-assemble cabinets

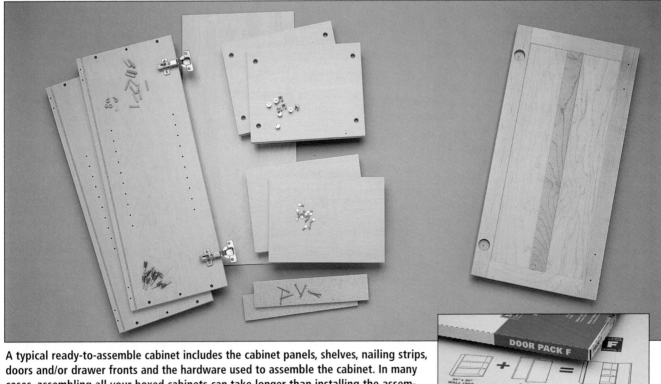

A typical ready-to-assemble cabinet includes the cabinet panels, shelves, nailing strips, doors and/or drawer fronts and the hardware used to assemble the cabinet. In many cases, assembling all your boxed cabinets can take longer than installing the assembled units. Cabinet doors on in-stock cabinets are normally sold in separate cartons coded to match the cabinet. Keep this in mind when purchasing cabinets and when estimating costs.

How to establish layout lines for base cabinets

Top line for cabinets
(34½ in. above high point of floor)

Stud locations

1 Find the high point of the floor next to the wall (or walls) where the cabinets will be installed. If you can't tell from a quick visual inspection, simply lay a long straight board on the floor along each wall. Level the board: if there is a high point, it will work as a fulcrum under the board. Mark the location of the high point on the wall, then measure up 34½ in. above the floor (for standard cabinets) at the high point and mark a reference point. Use a 4 ft. level to extend a reference line out in both directions from the point. Mark all walls that will support base cabinets. Also locate and mark wall framing members in the installation area. Use an electronic stud finder (See inset photo) to locate the framing members.

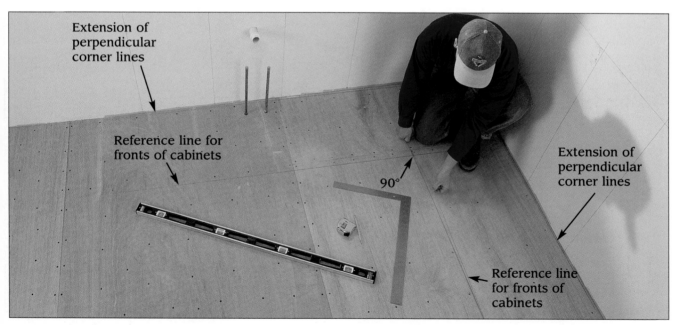

Extension of perpendicular corner lines

Reference line for fronts of cabinets

90°

Extension of perpendicular corner lines

Reference line for fronts of cabinets

2 Snap perpendicular reference lines to use as guides for positioning the fronts of the base cabinets. This can be a tricky process and the best way to do it depends on the plumbness of your walls and the direction, if any, they're out of alignment. In the example shown above, the room was very slightly out of square, splaying outward just a fraction from the corner. The walls were plumb (we tested with a level). In this case, perpendicular lines could be established at the corner using a framing square. The lines could then be extended with a chalkline. To establish the reference lines for the fronts of the cabinets (the points where the toekicks are attached) we simply measured the cabinets from back to front then measured out from the square corner lines that amount at several points in the cabinet installation area. Then, by snapping chalklines that connected these marks we were able to establish perpendicular reference lines for the fronts of the cabinets.

How to install base cabinets

1 Draw installation reference lines on the walls and floor (See previous page). If the end cabinet will butt up against a wall, begin installing base cabinets at the end of the run and use a scribe rail (See below). If the end cabinet is exposed and the layout is an "L"-shape, start in the corner. Position the corner cabinet so it's flush with the front reference lines. Check the sides for square with a framing square.

2 Lay a 4 ft. level across the top of the corner cabinet. Slip wood shims under the bottoms of the cabinet sides until the cabinet is level side to side and front to back. Install enough shims so each cabinet side is supported in at least three spots. If your cabinets have adjustable leveler feet (See photo, page 77), follow the manufacturer's instructions to level the cabinet.

How to make & use a scribe rail

A *scribe rail* (although misnamed—it's really a stile) is a filler strip that's tacked onto the outer edge of the face frame on an end cabinet. The width is determined by the size of the gap between the cabinet and the wall.

Make scribe rails and filler strips from the same material as the face frames. If you're ordering prefinished cabinets, make sure to order enough filler strips for your layout.

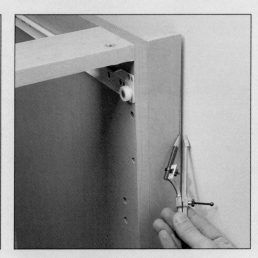

1 Make sure the end cabinet is parallel to the line formed by the cabinet bank, then measure the gap between the cabinet and the wall at its widest point. Rip a filler strip to this width.

2 Apply wood glue to the edge of the filler strip then clamp it to the outer edge of the face frame. Set the cabinet in position using temporary levels and shims. Use a compass to scribe the contour of the wall onto the scribe rail, setting the distance between the compass legs to equal the widest gap.

3 With a belt sander or plane, shape the edge to match the profile line (See page 86). Then, shape a slight bevel into the back edge of the rail to help it fit snugly against the wall.

3 Attach the leveled corner cabinet to the wall if it is a full-depth cabinet (some corner cabinets have a semicircular or shortened back panel that doesn't reach all the way to the corner—See next photo). Align the bottom of the cabinet with the perpendicular reference lines for the fronts of the cabinets. If the toekick area of the cabinet does not reach the line, shift it forward until it does. Slip wood shims between the upper rails at the back of the cabinet and the walls at screw locations then screw the cabinet to the wall using #8 × 3 in. wallboard screws.

VARIATION: For corner cabinets that are not full-depth, set the cabinet in place and level it, then install the base cabinets on each side. The corner cabinet is secured by attaching it to the adjoining cabinet sides or face frames (See next photo). With the cabinet leveled, cut nailing strips to attach to the wall at stud locations, level with the top of the cabinet. The cleats will provide support for the countertop.

OPTION FOR
CABINETS WITH FACE FRAMES

4 Drill countersunk pilot holes through each corner cabinet side and into the side of the neighboring cabinet. If your new cabinets have face frames, drill the countersunk pilot holes all the way through one face frame and well into the adjoining one (the pilot should be about 2½ in. deep if your face frames are each

1½ in. thick—right photo). Drive three wallboard screws through each cabinet side or face frame stile and into the adjacent cabinet to bind the corner cabinet to the other base cabinets. Screws should be ¼ in. shorter than the combined width of the two cabinet sides or face frames.

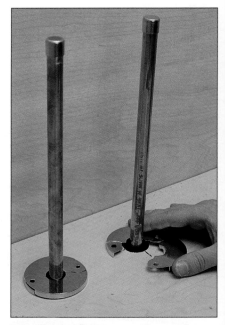

5 Install the sink base. Start by plotting the location of the water supply tubes and drain pipe onto the cabinet back or bottom. Use a hole saw to drill entry holes for the pipes. If the supply tubes and the drain pipe will enter the cabinet through the same panel (for example, if all three will enter in the back panel), you can make the holes so they're just slightly larger in diameter than the pipes they're drilled to accept. But if the pipes will enter the cabinet through more than one cabinet panel, drill the holes with ½ in. or more of extra clearance per hole to create some wiggle room for positioning the cabinet.

TIP: Slip pipe flanges over the supply tubes and drain pipe to cover the gaps in the cabinet openings. Used most frequently on exposed pipes, as with wall-hung or pedestal sinks, the flanges improve appearance and can limit entry points into a cabinet for insects or rodents.

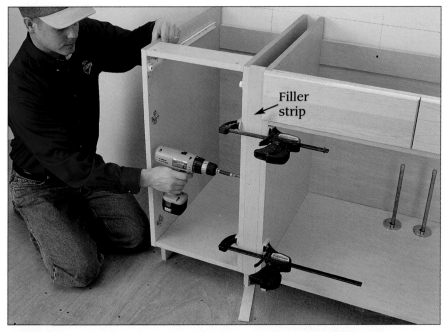

Filler strip

6 Install the remaining base cabinets. Cut filler strips to fit between cabinets as dictated by your layout plan. As you work, attach cleats at any countertop location where a cabinet is not installed (such as an opening for a dishwasher). For cabinets that have wide gaps at the walls because the room is out of square, cut spacer strips from ¼ in. plywood and slip them between the cabinet backs and wall at screw locations. Drive three or four 3 in. wallboard screws through the cabinet frame and into the wall studs. If necessary, back out the screws, relevel the cabinet, then redrive screws.

7 Install a kickplate to conceal the openings underneath the cabinets. You can purchase a kickplate from the cabinetry manufacturer, or cut one yourself from matching wood stock. Another option is to use a strip of ¼ in. plywood (such strips usually are painted black). Scribe the bottom of the kickplate to follow the floor line, then sand or plane it up to the scribe line. Finish to match, then attach with finish nails driven through the kickplate and into the ends of the cabinet sides. Set the nailheads and fill with tinted wood putty.

French cleat

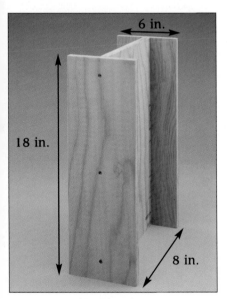

VARIATION:
The sequence that follows shows how to hang a wall cabinet by screwing directly through the cabinet frame at wall framing member locations. Another way to hang a cabinet is to use a system of "French cleats" where a cleat with an upward bevel is attached to the wall and a cleat with a downward bevel is attached to the cabinet. The cabinet cleat fits over the wall-mounted cleat.

How to hang wall cabinets

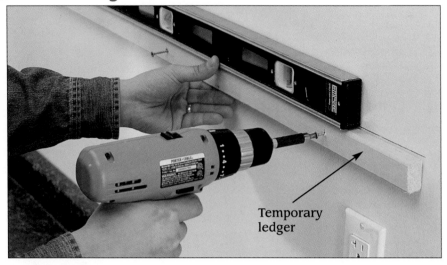

Temporary ledger

1 NOTE: There are at least two good reasons to install the countertop on the base cabinets before proceeding with the wall cabinet installation, as was done here: First, the countertop provides a bearing surface for resting cabinet jacks that support the wall cabinets during installation. Second, installing the countertop allows you to install the sink sooner, which can be a great relief if you're conducting a weekends-only kitchen remodeling project. Determine the best height for the upper cabinets. The bottoms should be at least 15 in. above the countertop; 18 in. is common. With 30-in. high cabinets, the cabinet tops generally are 84 in. above the floor. Measure up from the countertop or floor in several spots and make reference marks. Snap a chalkline or connect the marks with a straightedge. Then, level and tack a temporary 1 × 2 ledger to the wall. The ledger supports and aligns the cabinet bottoms.

TIP: Build a cabinet jack to support wall cabinets during installation. The jack shown above is made from plywood and dimensioned to support upper wall cabinets at the correct height when it's placed on the countertop below. If the wall-hung cabinets are not above a base cabinet, use a pair of 2 × 4s for temporary support.

2 Start the installation of wall-hung cabinets in the corner of an "L" or "U" layout. Diagonal corner cabinets, like the one shown above, are designed to fit snugly into the corner. Blind corner cabinets (See illustration, page 65) need to be positioned so the door will be the same distance from the corner created by the filler strip as it is from the door on the adjoining cabinet. Secure the corner cabinet in rough position, supporting it with the ledger and a jack from below.

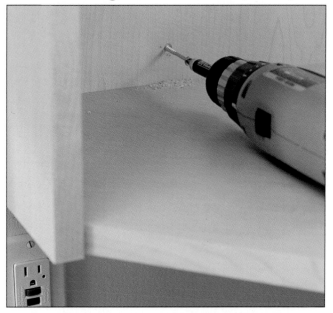

3 Adjust the position of the cabinet until it's level front to back and flush on top of the ledger. When the cabinet is in correct position, drive a pair of #8 × 3 in. screws through the cabinet back and into a wall stud location. The screws should be driven through frame strips at the top and bottom of the back panel. Drive the screws until they're just short of being snug so you can make minor adjustments to the cabinet.

4 Check the cabinet with a level to make sure it's plumb. If necessary, slip long wood shims between the cabinet and the wall. Once the cabinet is plumb, fully tighten the screws. Drive additional screws through the cabinet back at the location of framing members.

5 Get adjoining cabinets into rough position then clamp them to the corner cabinet. Drive screws partway through the back panel to steady each cabinet, then drive screws through the face frame or sides of the corner cabinet and into the adjoining cabinet (See step 4, page 69). Install all cabinets in the wall-hung cabinet bank. If necessary, add a scribe rail to end cabinets (See page 68). Hang doors and shelves.

Choosing hardware

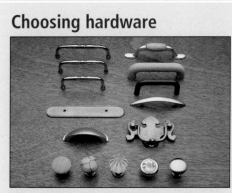

Door and drawer pulls and knobs have a great effect on the appearance of cabinets—old or new. To make an informed buying choice, pick out a few possibilities at the store and try them out on your cabinets first.

End panels

Many prefabricated cabinets manufactured today are not made with finished end panels on the sides (the assumption is that they will be stacked next to other cabinets so the end panels won't be visible anyway). To create a finished end panel, attach a piece of ¼ in. plywood of matching wood species and finish to the cabinet ends on each side of the opening. Use construction adhesive and small wire nails to attach the end panels. Generally, base cabinets have finished ends.

6 (Right) Install cabinet hardware, including hinges and pulls or knobs for drawers and doors. TIP: Clamp a long ledger to the cabinet bank (or rest it on the floor) and rest all the doors for a row of cabinets on the ledger when marking hinge positions. This ensures that the doors will be aligned. If you're installing unfinished cabinets, apply your finish of choice before hanging doors and attaching hardware.

TIP: Make a jig for cutting crown molding

The crown molding jig shown here "re-creates" the relationship of the cabinet face and a flat horizontal plane or the ceiling. By positioning a piece of crown molding so the back beveled edges are flush against the surfaces of the jig, you can make a straight, accurate miter cut.

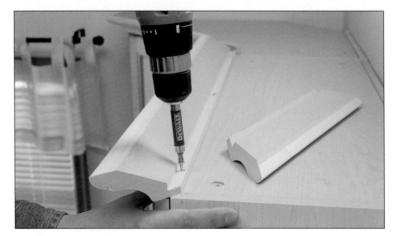

7 (OPTIONAL) Finish the tops by adding crown molding, if it is consistent with your cabinet style. Miter-cut the corners to fit around any exposed end cabinets. Many compound miter saws are built with positive stops for setting up to cut crown molding. Another way is to make a simple jig that holds the crown molding in the correct position against the saw fence while you make a 45° cut (See TIP, left).

Kitchen islands convert little-used space into valuable food preparation/dining areas. A custom countertop made from solid surfacing material gives this island a sturdy, expansive quality. The three pendant style lights place focus on the work area.

Kitchen islands

Island cabinets have become one of the most popular kitchen design elements in recent years, and for good reason. The kitchen island offers much greater versatility than the the old eat-in area or breakfast nook area that it has functionally replaced. Where the eat-in counters were pretty much limited to dining duty, the island countertop can be used either as an eating surface or as a food preparation area, owing to its accessibility from the other work areas of the room.

You don't need to have huge amounts of open floor space to create an island in your kitchen. If you've got about six feet of clear space from your kitchen counter or sink area to the opposite wall, you can install an island. Granted, it will be a small island and passage may get cozy at times, but it will fit (See illustration, right). You can make smaller islands more efficient by installing casters or making sure the island is lightweight enough to be moved easily. This way, you can position the island to increase or decrease the clear space in a selected traffic area.

Islands can be accessorized in many ways, including with built-in cooktops or sinks, or even hard-wired receptacle strips for small appliances.

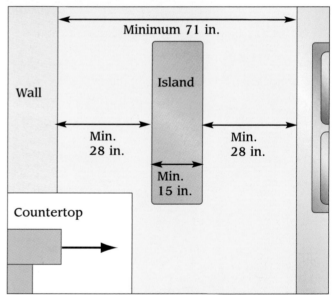

A minimum of 71 in. of clear space from counter edge to the nearest wall is needed to install a kitchen island. With this amount of space, you can just squeeze in a 15 in. wide island surface (pretty much the minimum useful size), with a minimal passing distance of 28 in. on each side of the island. When measuring the available space in your kitchen be sure to measure form the furthest projection of each element: for example, measure from the countertop edges, not the cabinets (inset).

Tips for designing kitchen islands

Experiment with shapes. Just as real islands are not rectangular or square, kitchen islands can be just about any shape. The rounded end of this countertop makes it possible to seat three people on stools without closing off the traffic lanes. A built-in cooktop with downdraft frees up valuable counter space.

Be creative with cabinets when building the island base. The two-level island shown here combines wall-hung and base cabinets in convincing fashion. The addition of a sink and the overhanging countertop add function to the visually appealing design.

How to install kitchen island cabinets

1 Some kitchen cabinet manufacturers make special island cabinets with pedestal bases and finished back panels, but an alternative to special-ordering these units is to use standard base cabinets to fashion a kitchen island. Start by setting the cabinets in position then tracing around the bases onto the floor. NOTE: Our plan called for an island with a countertop overhang for bar stools and a sink, so we used a sink base and a smaller base cabinet to create the cabinet base for the island.

2 Remove the cabinets, then measure inside the outlines and draw new outlines, subtracting the thickness of the cabinet sides. Cut 2 × 2 nailers to fit against the inside of the side walls and back of each cabinet (leave the front open). Attach the nailers to the floor with 3 in. deck screws.

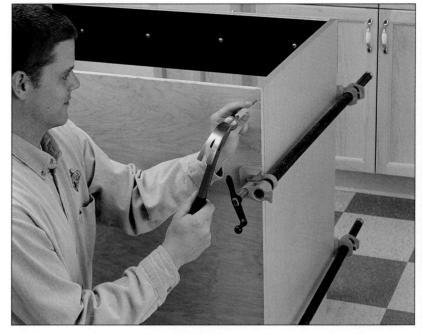

3 Set the cabinets over the nailers and shim to level. Drive screws through the adjoining sides on multiple-cabinet installations to draw the cabinets together. Double-check to make sure the cabinets are still level, then drive 8d finish nails through the cabinet sides and into the nailers. Set the nailheads with a nailset then fill the holes with wood putty.

4 Make a back panel for the island. If your base cabinets have face frames, create a frame-and-panel (or faux frame-and-panel) style back panel that mimics the look, proportions and face frame overhang amounts of the cabinet fronts. For our face-frameless cabinets, we simply cut a piece of ¾ in. thick maple plywood to fit flush with the outside faces of the island sides. We covered the plywood edges with maple veneer edge tape, then attached the back panel with glue and 8d finish nails.

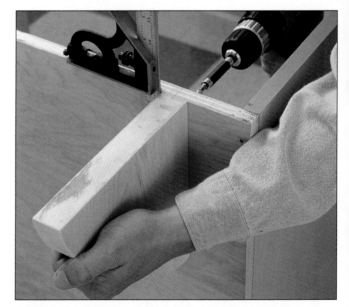

5 Attach a toekick strip across the toekick area at the cabinet fronts. If there are noticeable gaps around the outside edges of the cabinet, trim the gaps with quarter-round molding.

OPTION: If you have enough clear passage in your kitchen, consider overhanging the countertop at the edge to make a breakfast bar. Generally, a 12 in. overhang is the minimum overhang to accommodate bar stools. In most cases, it's a good idea to attach corbels (braces) to the cabinet to provide support for the countertop. For the island shown above, we planned to install a heavy poured concrete countertop (See pages 104 to 113), so we used 3 in. screws to attach 1½ × 10 × 12 in. maple corbels.

Bathroom cabinets

As more and more homes include expansive master bathroom suites, traditional kitchen-style cabinetry is showing up with greater frequency. In addition, manufacturers are increasing the number of styles and configurations for more standard bathroom cabinets, especially vanities and double vanities and etigierre (over-john) cabinets that are installed over the toilet area. Bathroom cabinets are distinguished from kitchen cabinets mostly by the fact that they're generally about 6 in. shorter. Whichever style you're installing, the techniques are virtually identical.

Cabinet leveler legs

Standard vanities are shorter than kitchen cabinets: usually 30 or 32 in. high, including the countertop thickness. But because most adults are more comfortable using a taller cabinet, manufacturers are beginning to make taller vanity cabinets. You can make a standard vanity taller by adding adjustable leveler legs to the base. Leveler legs (sold at most hardware and woodworking stores) usually come with a pair of clips so a toekick can be attached to the legs without fasteners. While this takes care of the front, it won't help conceal exposed sides. One way to solve this problem is to add 1 × 2 nailing strips to the inside of the base at the sides so you can attach scribed filler strips to the sides as well. The filler strips can be painted to match the toekick or veneered to match the cabinet.

How to install a vanity cabinet

1 Remove the old sink or vanity. Mark location lines for the cabinet. Start by marking the midpoint of the drain pipe location on the floor (ideally, the vanity will be centered under a recessed medicine cabinet, but it's more important that it be centered on the drain). Also make sure there is at least 12 in. of clear space if the vanity is next to a toilet. Measure out in both directions from the centerline to establish the locations for the vanity cabinet sides.

2 Set the vanity in place and test for level. If it's off by more than ¼ in. or so, reposition the cabinet and shim the sides until the top is level.

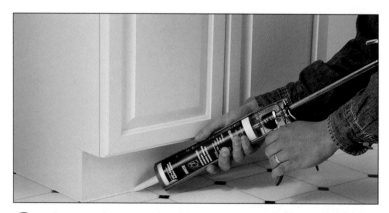

3 Anchor the cabinet by driving 3 in. screws through the top, back rail and into wall studs (See step 3, page 69). Attach a toekick if none is pre-attached (See step 7, page 70). Fill small gaps around the bottom of the vanity with caulk or conceal with quarter-round molding. Attach a countertop (See step 9, page 87) and drop-in sink or a premolded vanity top with integral sink. Hook up the sink (See page 121).

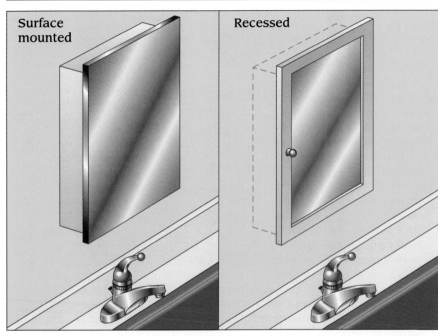

Surface mounted

Recessed

Traditionally, medicine cabinets are recessed into the bathroom wall above the sink or vanity (right). While this may offer some minor space-saving advantages, most home-owners and builders today prefer to install surface-mounted cabinets (left) and avoid cutting into the wall. Many new medicine cabinets can be installed either way.

Medicine cabinets

The medicine cabinet is one of the most used and most useful cabinets in just about every home. All you need to do is open one up and try to find a spot for your new can of shaving cream to realize exactly how heavily used the medicine cabinet is. For this reason, replacing an old, cramped medicine cabinet with a newer, more spacious model is a quick and easy remodeling project that offers instant rewards.

When selecting a medicine cabinet, the basic choice is between recessed and surface mounted (See left). Beyond that, you'll need to consider basic styling, the number of doors and whether or not it has a built-in light source (side lights are preferable to top mounted).

How to replace a recessed medicine cabinet

1 Remove the old medicine cabinet, then lay out the project area for the new cabinet. Mark cutting lines for the new wall opening. Center vertical lines at stud locations. If you will be cutting a wall stud, extend the lower cutting line so it's 1½ in. below the rough opening to allow for a 2 × 4 sill (if more than one stud will be cut, check with your local building department for sill and header thickness requirements).

2 Remove wall coverings in the project area. On wallboard walls, score along the cutting lines with a utility knife and straightedge, then pry out wallboard with a flat pry bar. On lathe-and-plaster walls, cut along cutting lines with a circular saw and straightedge guide. The saw blade should be set so it will cut about ⅛ in. deeper than the thickness of the wall covering. If your room has a nontextured wallboard ceiling, you may find it easier to patch in new wallboard if you remove old material all the way up to the ceiling.

3 Mark cutting lines on framing members in the project area. If cutting more than one stud, install temporary supports. Cut out sections of framing members in the project area, following the cutting lines. Use a reciprocating saw to make the cuts.

4 Frame the rough opening for the cabinet. Typically, the rough opening should be ½ to 1 in. larger than the cabinet in both directions to allow for leveling and shimming. Use 12d common nails or 3 in. wallboard screws to install framing members. TIP: Slip a spacer block between vertical framing members to provide support when driving screws or nailing toe-nail style.

Spacer block

5 Patch the wall with new wall covering material. Be sure to follow local codes when installing wallcovering materials in a wet area. NOTE: If you will be be doing any electrical work, it should be completed and inspected before you install the wall coverings. Tape and sand the patched area. In most cases, you'll want to paint or finish the wall before installing the medicine cabinet.

6 Install the medicine cabinet. Check with a level and shim as needed to make sure the cabinet is level and plumb. Unless the manufacturer's directions suggest another method, secure the cabinet with 16d casing nails or 2 in. wallboard screws driven through the cabinet sides and into the trimmer studs on the sides of the opening. Preattached trim molding should be flush against the wall surface. If the trim is not preattached, miter-cut case molding to fit and attach with finish nails.

Countertops

There is no such thing as a perfect countertop material. While there are many suitable materials from which you can fashion a kitchen counter or a bathroom vanity top, each has its own strengths and drawbacks. Take ceramic tile, for example. A popular countertop option these days, ceramic tile is highly attractive, available in a wide range of colors and styles and can be installed by just about anyone with a little bit of do-it-yourself ability. But on the negative side, the higher-end quality tiles are fairly expensive (and naturally these are the ones we always choose first at the tile store); the grout lines between tiles can allow water penetration; and the tile surface itself is hard to the point of being unforgiving (you don't need to knock over your favorite coffee mug too many times to find this out).

Nevertheless, by making a careful evaluation of your needs and tastes you can find the countertop solution that works best for you and your budget. It may mean compromising your favorite look for a little more durability, or downgrading an appliance choice to create some extra room in your budget, but spend some time and employ some creative thought before making this important kitchen or bathroom updating decision.

If you are conducting a large remodeling project, wait as long as you can before installing the new countertops. Most countertop materials are relatively delicate and difficult to repair if they're damaged while you work on other parts of the room. But keep in mind that one of the most important functions of a countertop, be it in a bathroom or kitchen, is to support the sink, so if you're anxious to revive your supply of fresh water, go ahead and install the countertop as soon as the base cabinets are in.

Design tips for choosing countertops

Don't skimp on quality, especially when dealing with relatively small countertops, as with the vanity top shown here. When made from a long-lasting building material, like the solid surfacing material shown here and on page 103, countertops can easily stand up to moisture and heavy use for decades.

Be creative with the backsplash. A standard backsplash is between 4 and 5 inches high. But by extending the backsplash material all the way to the bottoms of the upper cabinets, the designer of this room enhanced the extravagant, monolithic appearance of the countertops, simplifying the lines in the process.

Strive for warmth. Because the kitchen naturally becomes a gathering place for families and guests (whether you want it to or not) look for products and design ideas that convey a feeling of warmth and welcome, as the rustic tile countertops do in the photo above. Keep in mind that even cool colors can convey "warmth" with texture and creative application.

Postform

- **Durability: Okay**; minimal seams reduce water penetration but thin surface coating is vulnerable to scratching and other forms of damage
- **Cleanability: Good**; hard washable surface with minimal seams and gaps
- **Heat resistance: Low**
- **Style variety: Low** (but can be custom-ordered in many colors and styles)
- **Cost: Low to medium**

Postform countertops are made from sections of particleboard with preattached laminated surfaces and integral backsplashes. Postform pieces are carried in-stock at most building centers in various lengths and standard countertop width (25½ in.). Premitered sections are generally sold as well, along with straight sections that have no backsplash. Postform is the cheapest common countertop material and is very easy to install. The primary drawback is in selection: most building centers will carry only a couple of colors and styles in stock. But if you can wait a few weeks, there is almost no limit to the colors and patterns, as well as the size, that can be custom-ordered. See pages 84 to 87.

Plastic laminate

- **Durability: Okay**; little water penetration on surface, but can be vulnerable at edges and back; generally has a harder surface than postform
- **Cleanability: Good**; gap at backsplash can create problems if not well caulked; some textures streak easily
- **Heat resistance: Low**
- **Style variety: High**
- **Cost: Low to medium**

Plastic laminate has endured an undeservedly bad reputation at times because it tends to be confused with lower-grade tileboard that was designed for shower stalls and other vertical applications but is often misused as an inexpensive countertop or tabletop material. Real plastic laminate is made by impregnating layers of kraft paper under pressure with plastic resin to form a hard, durable substrate. A paper color/pattern layer is bonded to the substrate, then coated with a layer of protective clear melamine to complete the manufacturing process. The plastic laminate is glued to a subbase of particleboard or medium-density fiberboard. It is available in dozens of styles, patterns and textures. See pages 88 to 95.

Ceramic tile

- **Durability: Good**; tiles themselves are very durable but grout joints can be problematic; some risk of cracking
- **Cleanability: Okay**; smooth glazed tiles clean up well, although grout lines don't; cleanability decreases as texture increases
- **Heat resistance: High**
- **Style variety: Medium**
- **Cost: Medium to high**

Ceramic tile is a truly unique material when used for countertop installations. The individual tiles can be positioned to adapt to just about any shape or size, yet when the surface is completed it has a monolithic quality as if it were fashioned from a single piece of tile. Use thicker floor tiles for kitchen countertops. For bathroom vanities and noncountertop surfaces you can use thinner (cheaper) wall tiles. Avoid mosaic sheets for countertop applications since the small size of the individual tiles results in too many vulnerable grout lines. Also avoid larger 12 × 12 tiles, which can result in awkward shapes and irregular grout lines. For most applications, 4 × 4, 6 × 6 or 8 × 8 tiles are best. See pages 96 to 102.

Solid surfacing material

- Durability: **High**
- Cleanability: **High** (scratches can be sanded out)
- Heat resistance: **Good**
- Style variety: **Limited but improving**
- Cost: **High**

Solid surfacing material for countertops is known best by its popular brand names, particularly Corian by DuPont. Other brand names include Avonite, Gibraltar, Surell and Swanstone. Formed by binding resins and natural minerals together under heat and pressure, countertops made from solid surface materials will stand up to all types of abuse, while offering a seamless, high-end appearance. But they are quite costly and manufacturers of the solid surfacing panels do not recommend that homeowners work the material themselves. In fact, most factory warranties require that the product be installed by a certified technician. See page 103.

Poured concrete

- Durability: **Depends on quality of installation and other variables; if properly installed can last for generations**
- Cleanability: **Okay; when troweled smooth and sealed will resist staining, otherwise can absorb stains**
- Heat resistance: **High**
- Style variety: **Medium**
- Cost: **Low (materials only)**

Poured concrete is not traditionally counted among the most desirable countertop building materials, but that is changing quickly. While it has been employed as counter and table-top material for centuries in some parts of the world, it is just beginning to gain acceptance here in the United States. When pigmented and properly troweled to a smooth, deep finish concrete can offer advantages no other material can claim: it is truly seamless and it is, literally, as hard as rock. But the success of this material depends entirely on the manner in which it is installed. A good job will create a counter that will last indefinitely; a poorly installed countertop can crack and crumble almost immediately. See pages 104 to 113.

Other countertop materials

The countertop types featured in this section represent the most common selections for building your own kitchen cabinet countertops and vanity tops. But there are numerous other materials that have been adapted for use as countertops, and some quite successfully. Here are a few additional countertop material options you may want to consider:

Wood (Butcher block): Because it is not water-resistant, wood is seldom used to make countertops anymore—especially in areas near sinks and other sources of water and heat. But in the right spot (for example, a kitchen island with no sink or cooktop cutout) a butcher block top can provide an unmatched blend of warmth, style and function.

Stainless steel: A very common countertop surface in commercial applications, stainless steel is one of the hottest materials in residential kitchen design. The advantages are many, particularly when it comes to hygiene and dramatic contemporary styling. But it is a very expensive material that must be custom-fabricated by a professional.

Natural stone tile: Has most of the same advantages and disadvantages as ceramic tile, but tends to create uneven surfaces that create awkward situations. But on the positive side, in the right spot natural stone can outclass any other building material on sheer appearance.

Cultured marble: A very common surface material used mostly to make vanity tops with integral sinks.

Granite or marble slabs: If you can afford them, these monolithic countertops are the absolute top of the line.

Postform countertops are inexpensive and easy to install. With a built-in backsplash and minimal or no seams, they're also low maintenance and long-lasting. And they're available in a wider range of colors and styles than ever before.

Postform countertops don't require a subbase: they rest directly on particleboard build-up strips that are tacked to the tops of the cabinet sides. The countertop is secured by driving screws up through the build-up strips where possible, and through blocking at the top corners of the cabinet cases.

Integral backsplash

Build-up strip

Mid-run cabinet side

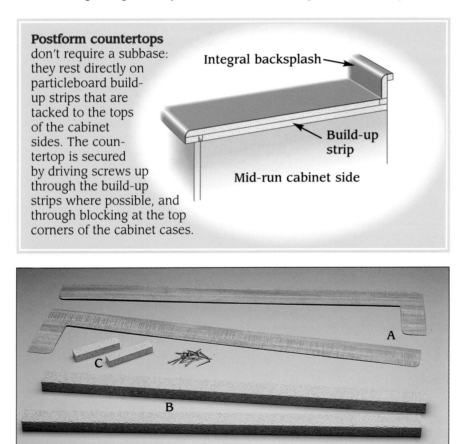

End-cap kits for finishing exposed postform ends include: matching laminate profiled to cover the backsplash and the countertop edge (A); build-up strips that are glued to the underside of the countertop before the end caps are attached (B); and small filler strips that fit along the ends of the backsplash (C).

Countertops
Postform

If you're looking for a reasonably attractive new countertop that's inexpensive and easy to install, postform may be just the material for you. Postform is prefabricated, laminated particleboard assembled and cut into various stock countertop sizes and configurations. The in-stock selection of colors and styles is very limited, but you can purchase postform custom-made for your dimensions and with a laminate color and style of your choosing. If you're ordering in postform, be sure to take careful measurements of the countertop: with correct sizes, the manufacturer or cabinetmaker can make miter cuts for countertop corners.

Unlike plastic laminate, the laminate layer on postform is constructed with the resin fibers all running in the same direction. This allows the laminate to be bent at relatively sharp angles to follow the rounded front edge profile and the integral backsplash.

How to install a postform countertop

1 Cut 2 in. wide strips of ¾ in. thick particleboard and tack them to the tops of the base cabinets with #6 × 1¼ in. wallboard screws.

2 Cut the countertop material to length, with the finished surface facing down. Draw cutting lines, then cut with a circular saw and crosscutting or panel-cutting blade. Following a straightedge cutting guide, cut up to the backsplash. Finish the cut through the backsplash using a jig saw. Make miter cuts at 45°. If your walls are not exactly perpendicular make up the variation when scribing the backsplash (See steps 5 to 6).

3 Attach premolded end caps to exposed countertop ends that are not mitered (See photo, previous page bottom). Attach the build-up and filler strips first, using glue and finish nails driven through pilot holes. Then, apply the end cap laminate strips to the countertop ends using glue. Some strips have a heat sensitive backing that is activated by ironing the laminate with a household iron at low heat setting. If the laminate strip is wider than the countertop thickness, align the strip with the bottom edge of the countertop and trim off the excess (See next step).

4 Trim the top edge of the laminate end caps so they're flush with the postform surface. For neatest results, use a router with a flush-trimming laminate bit (inset photo). A file may be used instead. Set the countertop sections in position on the cabinets so you can make sure they fit and mark the backsplash if it needs to be trimmed to fit flush against the walls.

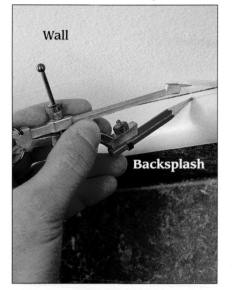

5 Apply masking tape to the top of the backsplash to create a surface for marking. Set the legs of a compass with a pencil in one leg to match the width of the widest gap between the backsplash and the wall. Then, scribe the profile of the wall onto the top of the backsplash (See page 68 for more description of this technique).

6 Remove the countertop sections and set them on a worksurface so you have clear access to the backsplash. Use a belt sander with 50-grit sanding belt to pare the back edge of the backsplash to follow the scribed wall profile line. Remove tape and clean up the sanded edge with a file if necessary. If you don't own a belt sander, try using a block plane to pare to the cutting line.

7 If you've purchased pre-mitered countertop sections, like those shown here, simply apply glue along the joint, press the sections together upside-down on a flat surface, then insert mechanical fasteners at the premortised locations. Tighten the fasteners enough to draw the sections together, but do not fully tighten them yet. If you're cutting your own miters, use a straightedge guide and cut with a circular saw and jig saw (See step 2). It's important to get a clean cut for a smooth seam, so use a very sharp blade (a hollow-ground planer blade is a good choice for the circular

saw portion of the cut). Unless the cut is exceptionally straight and clean, it's a good idea to go over it with a belt sander and 100-grit paper to smooth it out. Make a template and use a router with a straight bit to cut the mortises. Or, use a drill and a wood chisel. Join the sections as described for the premitered sections.

8 Lay a wood block across the seam and tap it with a mallet to even out the two halves of the joint. Tighten the mechanical fasteners securely, checking to make sure the two halves of the countertop remain aligned.

9 Attach the countertop by driving #6 × 1¼ in. wallboard screws up through the particleboard build-up strips and into the underside of the countertop at 12 to 24 in. intervals. If your cabinets have flat frame rails like those shown in the photo to the right, drive screws through these rails and into the counter-top. Also drive screws at the corners of the cabinets (use corner blocks if necessary).

10 Apply clear silicone caulk along the top edge of the backsplash at the wall joint. TIP: To protect the backsplash and the wall, apply tape to both, leaving a narrow gap over the seam. Caulk the gap carefully then wipe off the excess caulk with a damp cloth or a moistened finger (try to create a slightly concave profile in the caulk). Carefully remove the tape before the caulk sets.

11 Lay out cutouts for sink (and cook-top if installing a separate cooktop). Use the template provided by the sink manufacturer if you can, otherwise create the cutout so it's about ½ in. wider and deeper than the body of the sink under the rim (See pages 120 to 122 for more on sink installations). Protect the postform surface by applying masking tape over the cutting lines. If the tape obscures the lines, redraw them on top of the tape. Make sure the cutout doesn't bite into the front buildup strip. Tack sturdy wood scraps over the cut-lines at each side of the cutout to support the waste piece so it doesn't fall out pre-maturely and cause the countertop surface to splinter (attach the scraps in the waste area only). Make the cutout with a jig saw.

Supports (attach to waste area only)

Plastic laminate offers a host of advantages for countertop construction. And as it has grown in popularity, the variety of colors, textures and patterns has increased dramatically. From deep, rich textured colors like the surface above to faux marble or wood, you can find a laminate to accomplish just about any decorative goal.

Countertops
Plastic laminate

Plastic laminate is the most popular countertop surfacing material today. The reasons for its popularity are simple: it is relatively easy to work with, it provides a very durable and easy to clean surface and it is less expensive than most other countertop materials. It is also available in a vast array of colors, patterns and textures: from plain white to vivid, sophisticated reproductions of exotic wood grains and fine travertine.

Most building centers carry a limited selection of plastic laminate, along with a chip book of special-order types. But the bulk of the plastic laminate sold today is purchased through distributors that stock a nearly complete selection of whichever product line they feature. Look in your telephone directory under "Counters" or "Countertops" to find distributors in your area.

Typical plastic laminate for countertops is 1/16 in. thick. It can be ordered in a few standard lengths from 60 to 144 in., and in widths of 24, 36, 48 or 60 in. For standard (26 in. deep) countertops, you'll want to order the 36 in. wide material. The extra laminate can be used to edge the front and sides of the countertop, and you should even have enough left over to make a backsplash as well. While plastic laminate is a relatively inexpensive product, it's worth taking the time to find out the available sizes at your local distributor (you'll need to tell them which style you're interested in so they can check

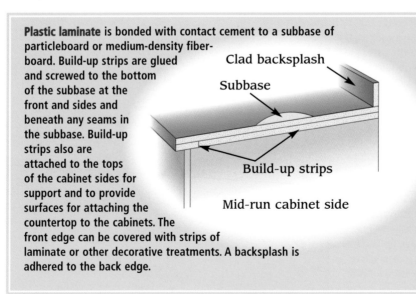

Plastic laminate is bonded with contact cement to a subbase of particleboard or medium-density fiberboard. Build-up strips are glued and screwed to the bottom of the subbase at the front and sides and beneath any seams in the subbase. Build-up strips also are attached to the tops of the cabinet sides for support and to provide surfaces for attaching the countertop to the cabinets. The front edge can be covered with strips of laminate or other decorative treatments. A backsplash is adhered to the back edge.

Clad backsplash

Subbase

Build-up strips

Mid-run cabinet side

what they have on hand) and drawing a plan. Be sure to take into account the planning guidelines presented in the diagram at right.

The majority of plastic laminate sold today is constructed in essentially the same manner. A backing of resin-impregnated paper gives the laminate its thickness and strength. A color layer or pattern layer, usually made of paper, is bonded to the laminate. Then, a coating of clear melamine is applied over the color layer to create a wear layer that resists moisture and damage from scratching or impact.

Applying plastic laminate is definitely one of those handyman skills that improves quickly once you have a project or two under your belt. From that standpoint, it's probably worth asking at your distributor if they have some cutoff pieces they'll give you so you can practice the basic skills first. If so, try as many of the cutting methods as you can (See page 91) and see which one yields the best results. Experiment with coverage amounts for the contact cement to get the feel for how much is too much and how much is not enough. But the most important skill to practice is trimming the laminate after it's applied to a subbase. The fastest way to judge the quality of any laminate installation is to examine the nose of the countertop.

Substrates for plastic laminate: Most professional countertop installers use ordinary particleboard as a base for their laminate countertops. Particleboard is stable, smooth and relatively inexpensive. But it is susceptible to chipping and will not stand up to moisture. Medium-density fiberboard is very similar to particleboard, but it is somewhat denser, less prone to chipping and can be machined more readily to create unusual shapes. Do not use plywood or waferboard as a substrate: the rough surfaces and coarse edges are not well suited for laminating.

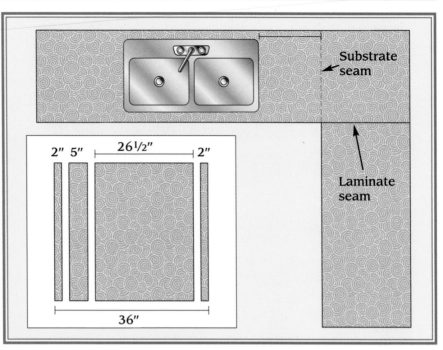

Planning your plastic laminate countertop project: For kitchen and bathroom countertops, 36 in. wide laminate can be used very efficiently. The substrate for the laminate is normally 25½ in. wide (in fact, you can buy particleboard precut to this dimension at countertop materials distributors). Allowing ½ in. overhang for trimming on each side, covering the surface of the substrate requires a 26½ in. wide piece. You'll also need a 2 in. wide strip for the front edge (to be trimmed to 1½ in. after application); and if you're making a backsplash you'll need additional strips of about 5 in. and 2 in. Allowing for cutting kerfs, this will allow you to barely squeeze out these four strips from one 36 in. wide strip of laminate (So cut carefully!). In most cases, it's easier to make seams at corners at right angles than to miter-cut the laminate. Just make sure the laminate seam is not directly over the substrate seam.

Tools and materials for working with plastic laminate include: contact cement—the nonflammable types are better in an enclosed area, while the original oil-based contact cement tends to provide a slightly stronger bond (A); a rubber J-roller for smoothing out the laminate (B); a paint roller with a short-nap adhesive sleeve for applying contact cement to broad surfaces (C); a flush-trimming laminate bit for router (D); sample chips for choosing color and style (E); disposable bristle brush for applying contact cement to smaller surfaces (F).

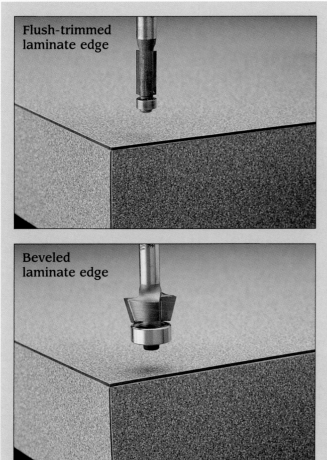

Flush-trimmed laminate edge

Beveled laminate edge

Finish treatments for laminate

One advantage to building your own countertop is that you can choose whichever edge and backsplash style you prefer. Among the more popular edge treatments are laminating the edges and shaping a flush seam or a decorative beveled seam, and attaching hardwood strips to the edge. A profile can be cut into the hardwood edge strip with a router to enhance the decorative effect.

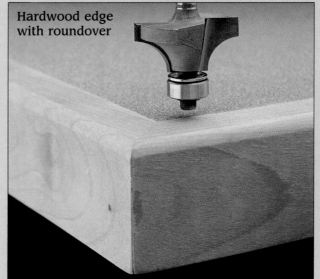

Hardwood edge with roundover

Backsplash options

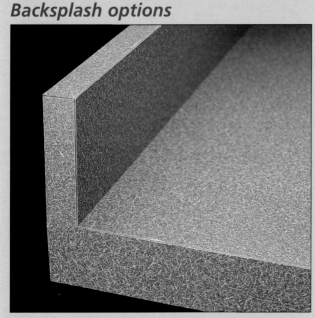

A strip of particleboard clad with the same laminate used on the countertops is the most basic backsplash option. Apply the tops and side pieces first, trim to fit, then apply the front strip. Trim and attach to countertop or wall with silicone adhesive.

A slight cant can be created simply by building tapered edges for the backsplash sides and bevel-ripping the bottom of the assembly to a low angle (8 to 10°). For best results, bevel-rip the top to the same angle. Then, simply apply the laminate as with a straight backsplash.

Cutting laminate

Much like veneer, plastic laminate is fairly fragile and delicate before it is applied to a subbase and must be cut with care. The most common methods for cutting are facedown on a table saw, faceup and cut with a circular saw, or scoring with a utility knife then snapping as you would cut wallboard.

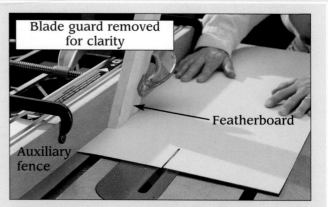

Blade guard removed for clarity

Featherboard

Auxiliary fence

Table saw (above). Before cutting laminate faceup on your table saw, attach an auxiliary fence flush with the tabletop so the laminate won't slide or wedge under the fence. A laminate-cutting blade prevents chipping of the surface.

Circular saw (above). The laminate should be facedown on a scrapwood cutting surface. Apply masking tape over the cutting line on the "good" side to protect the laminate surface, then clamp a straightedge guide to the laminate and cut with a small-tooth panel-cutting blade in your saw.

Score and snap (right). To cut narrow or delicate strips of laminate, score along the cutting line with a sharp utility knife, following a straightedge. If necessary, make multiple passes to achieve a groove that cuts through the wear layer and into the backing. Wearing gloves, set the laminate on a board so the score aligns with the edge and snap down sharply.

How to install a plastic laminate countertop

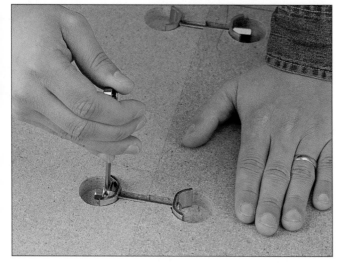

1 Make the subbase. Your local laminate distributor likely stocks ¾ in. particleboard in 25½ in. width (standard countertop width) and lengths of 4, 8 or 12 ft. Otherwise, rip a full sheet to this width on your table saw or with a panel cutter. Cut the subbase sections to length—they should overhang any exposed ends the same amount as the front (usually 1½ in.). Make straight butt joints at corners, not miters, and assemble the joints with mechanical fasteners and glue, as shown above.

2 Cut and attach 3 in. wide build-up strips to the underside of the subbase, flush with the front and side edges. Use 1¼ in. wallboard screws and glue. Work carefully, making sure the build-up strips are exactly flush with one another and there are no gaps at the vertical seams. NOTE: If you're planning to use hardwood or any countertop edging material other than laminate bonded directly to the subbase, skip to step 8.

3 Flip the subbase material so the top is facing up and support it from below with sawhorses. Prepare the edges for the glue bond by sanding or scraping down any projections in the front or side edges. Fill gaps with wood filler, then sand smooth. Wipe clean with a damp cloth and let the edges dry completely.

4 Laminate the countertop edges first (this should include all exposed ends as well as edges next to ovens or dishwashers where the countertop stops then starts again). Cut 2 in. wide strips of laminate about 1 in. longer than the countertop depth to cover any exposed sides. With a disposable paintbrush, apply a thin to medium-thick layer of contact cement to the side edges and to the backs of the laminate strips. Let the cement dry (See manufacturer's dry time recommendations). Because particleboard is an absorbent material, you'll get a better bond if you apply a second thin coat of cement.

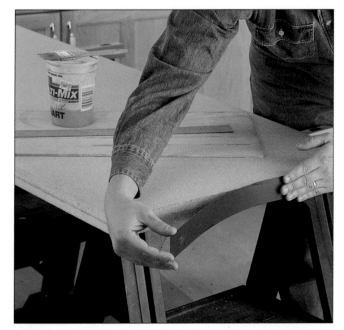

5 When the contact cement on the subbase and on the laminate has dried to the touch, press the laminate onto the subbase edge. Do this carefully, since the laminate is very difficult to remove or move once it has bonded. The laminate should overhang the sides, top and bottom. Roll with a J-roller.

6 Install a flush-cutting laminate trim bit in your router or laminate trimmer and rout around the perimeter of the laminate so it's flush with the surface of the subbase on sides, the top and the bottom. If your countertop has more than one exposed end, laminate all of them at this time.

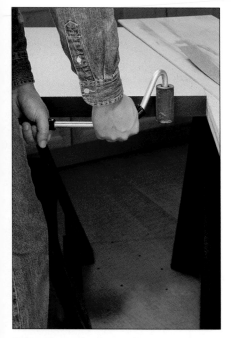

7 Laminate the front edges. Cut 2 in. wide strips of laminate to cover the front edges of the countertop. If possible, cut strips that are long enough to avoid any vertical seams. Attach the laminate to the front edges and trim to flush as with with side strips. The ends of the front strips should overhang the laminate at the sides of the countertop.

8 Apply laminate to the surface of the countertop. Cut the laminate so it overhangs the sides, back and front by about ½ in. (no overhang is necessary on the back edge if you'll be installing a backsplash). Lay the laminate upside down on the floor. Vacuum both the subbase surface and the back of the laminate. Apply contact cement to the subbase and the underside of the laminate, using a paint roller and short-nap adhesives sleeve. After a second, light coat has dried on the subbase, lay spacers (we used strips of cutoff wood) across the countertop at 12 in. intervals. The spacers will allow you to lay the laminate on top of the subbase and roughly position it without the two parts coming in contact.

9 Carefully lay the laminate sheet onto the spacers and arrange it with appropriate overhangs. The front edge of the laminate should be parallel to the front edge of the subbase (especially important if you're seaming the laminate). Remove the spacer on one end and press the laminate in place. Remove additional spacers in succession, pressing the laminate down as you go.

10 After all spacers are removed, roll the laminate thoroughly with a J-roller, rolling from the middle of the countertop and toward the edges. Be careful not to snap the overhang as you approach the edges.

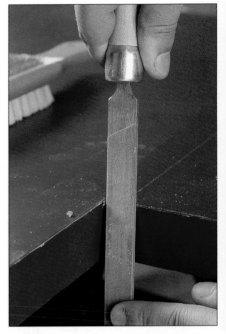

11 Repeat steps 9 and 10 to apply laminate to the remaining sections of the countertop. Start setting the new sheets against the old at butt seams. To ensure a tight seam, some installers recommend trimming the mating edges with a flush trimmer before glue is applied. Roll, then trim the edges.

12 Trim around the edges of the laminate so they're flush with the subbase. In inside corners (where the laminate bit can't reach) use a fine file to trim the laminate down.

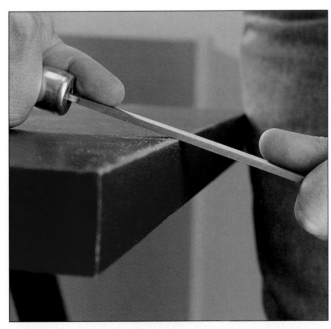

13 Chamfer the top edge all around the countertop using a chamfer bit or 7-to-15°-bevel laminate trim bit. Or, make two passes with a file: a shallow pass cutting downward slightly, then a steeper pass. In either case, do not cut into the vertical laminate on the edges: chamfer the edge of the top piece only.

14 Make the backsplash (See options, page 90). If your backsplash will be attached to the counter, install it before installing the countertop. If your backsplash material will be attached to the wall only, install the countertop first (for most installations, it's recommended that you attach the backsplash after the countertop is secured in position).

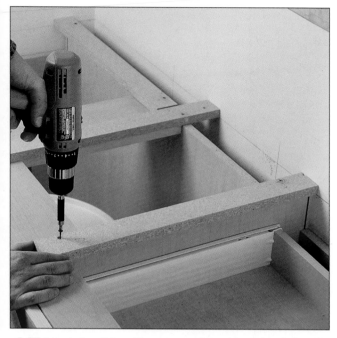

15 Attach 1 to 2 in. wide spacer strips to the tops of the cabinets, except on the outside edges of the two outer cabinets. The strips should stop short so they don't hit the front edge build-up strip. Depending on your cabinet structure, you may need to install corner blocks for attaching the countertop at this point. Many countertops can be attached simply by screwing up through the spreaders at the front and back of the cabinet.

16 With a helper, lift the countertop onto the base cabinets. Adjust it until it's in position and check with a level. Attach the countertop by driving screws up through the spreaders or corner blocks on the base cabinets. Double-check your screw length to avoid pop-outs.

17 Apply adhesive caulk to the reverse side of the backsplash (See step 14) and to the back edge of the countertop. Set the backsplash in position. Clamp a 2 × 4 to the front edge of the cabinet, then wedge pieces of 2 × 4 or 2 × 2 lumber between the backsplash and the front "rail" to hold the backsplash in place as the adhesive sets. Also apply padded clamps at the ends if you can reach them to seat the backsplash into the caulk bed on the countertop. Slip wood blocks between upper cabinets and the top of the backsplash, if possible, for the same purpose. After the adhesive has set, clean the countertop with the cleaner recommended by the contact cement manufacturer. Apply clear silicone caulk at the joint between the backsplash and the countertop and between the top of the backsplash and the wall. Install the sink and other appliances (See pages 120 to 122).

Ceramic tile countertops are elegant and very durable. They also resist heat quite well and have a customized appearance that adds unique character to a kitchen or bathroom. And with the countless sizes, colors and styles made at any given time, you can achieve just about any design goal you desire with tiles.

Countertops
Ceramic tile

Ask anyone to describe his or her "Dream Kitchen" and more often than not one of the first elements mentioned is "tile countertops." While ceramic tile may or may not be the ultimate countertop material, it does carry with it a certain mystique and sense of sophistication that, for many people, more than make up for its hardness and high level of maintenance. But one of the most attractive features of tile countertops is that installing one is a very manageable project for a typical do-it-yourselfer.

Ceramic tile is available in many sizes and shapes, but not all are suitable for making kitchen countertops. Wall tile is used frequently for countertops in both kitchen and bathroom. While it is inexpensive and easy to cut due to its thin profile, it is also relatively fragile and will not put up much of a fight if a pan or skillet is dropped onto it. For that reason, we recommend wall tiles for use only as a bathroom countertop material. For kitchens, you're better off using floor tiles, which at ¼ in. to ⅜ in. thick are

about twice as thick as typical ceramic wall tiles. The initial cost will be somewhat higher, but the heavier tiles are less likely to crack from impact or from movement of the subbase caused by exposure to moisture. The downside of floor tile (in addition to the cost and the difficulty cutting them) is that most floor tiles made today are 12 or 13 in. square. The larger size speeds up installation and results in fewer grout lines (grout lines are the single greatest weakness of tile countertops), but big tiles often result in irregular layout patterns as the difference between whole tiles and cut tiles is exaggerated. But don't rule larger tiles out, especially if

The subbase for a tile countertop is more complex than for most other countertop materials, but far less time consuming to create than the solid mortar beds used in the old days. Today, most installers employ ¾ in. thick exterior plywood as a base, then bond sheets of ⁵⁄₁₆ in. thick cementboard to the plywood with a layer of thinset mortar. Then another, thicker layer of thinset is applied to the cementboard and the tile is set into this layer. Finally, grout is used to fill the gaps between tiles.

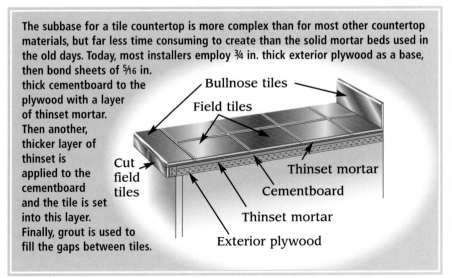

you have the flexibility to design your countertop to accommodate the tile dimensions. On the other end of the floor tile spectrum are mosaic sheets of tiles less than 2 in. square. While these are also easy to install and can look attractive, they result in too much countertop being covered with grout lines, which can lead to excessive water penetration and premature failure of the grout lines. For ease of installation, flexibility and appearance, floor tiles that are 6 or 8 in. square are the best bet when tiling countertops. While the selection you'll find may be somewhat limited (you'll have better luck at a tile shop than a typical building center), you can usually find a style and color that will work for you. If not, many tile shops allow you to custom-order tiles to your specifications.

In addition to the basic type, style and color, you should also think about the availability of non-field tiles when considering your countertop tile purchase. At the very minimum, the style you choose should have a matching bullnose tile. With field and bullnose you can tile just about any surface. But preferably, the tile will also have countertop edging (generally called "sink rail") or similar shapes (for example, "cap rail" or "C-cap" or "V-rail"). Some styles will have backsplash tiles with premolded coves on the bottom and a bullnose edge on top. Whichever styles you're considering, ask the salesperson to show you all the shapes and sizes it comes in. And use your creativity: there are many ways to combine tiles to make a suitable countertop.

In the old days, tile countertops generally were set onto a cast-in-place mortar base that was 2 in. thick or even heavier. There are still advantages to this kind of installation, but most installers today prefer to set countertop tile onto a subbase of thinset mortar applied over cementboard, with everything resting on exterior plywood.

A sampling of tile styles is all you can reasonably expect to find at any building center or even tile shop. Specific styles, colors, shapes and sizes vary greatly according to your region of the country and current design trends. In most cases, however, you can find 4¼ in. wall tile with matching bullnose tiles and perhaps sink rail and backsplash tiles like those used to make the white countertop section above. Floor tiles are fairly hit-or-miss as far as shape and size selection, but you can usually manage to find some combination that will make a pleasing countertop.

Tools and materials for installing a tile countertop include: tile cutter (A); notched trowel (B); grout sealer (C); grout float (D); grout (E); latex grout additive (F); thinset mortar (G); grout sponge (H); cementboard (I); fiberglass seam tape (J); tile spacers (K); rod saw for cutting tiles (L); and tile nippers (M).

Options for tile countertop edge treatments

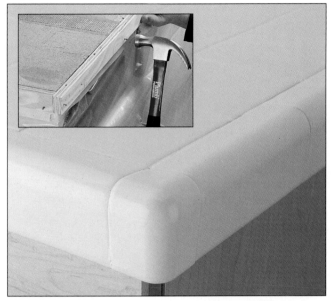

Matching tiles. Whether you use strips of field or bullnose tiles or special edging tiles, like the sink rail tiles shown above, a durable, tiled countertop edge blends perfectly with the countertop (although the grout lines often are mismatched). To create a sturdy base for the edge tiles, attach a buildup strip that's flush with the top of the cementboard tiling surface (inset photo).

Hardwood edging. This is the cheaper (depending on wood species) and easier way to edge a tile countertop. But it is also less durable. The edging should be applied before the tile is installed, then protected with masking tape during installation. Miter exposed corners.

How to use a tile cutter

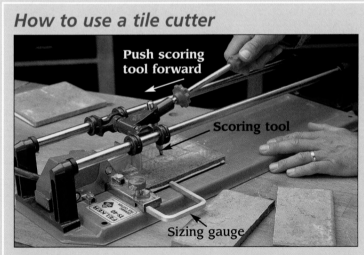

Push scoring tool forward

Scoring tool

Sizing gauge

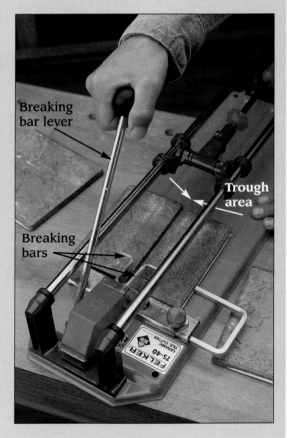

Breaking bar lever

Trough area

Breaking bars

1 (Above) Set the tile on the bed of the tile cutter so the cutting line is aligned with the point of the scoring tool. Some tile cutters, like the one above, are equipped with a sizing gauge so you can set the tool to make multiple cuts that are the same width. Lighter duty cutters often cut on the pull stroke, but the rented, heavy-duty model shown here cuts on the push stroke. Press down on the lever that lowers the scoring tool and push forward, scoring the cutting line.

2 (Right) Retract the scoring tool clear of the tile, then lower the lever that controls the breaking bars. These bars exert downward pressure toward the trough in the center of the bed, causing the tile to snap along the scored line.

How to install a ceramic tile countertop

1 Cut the subbase to size from ¾ in. exterior-rated plywood. Allow for the thickness of the build-up strip on the front edge, if you plan to use tile to edge the countertop. The subbase and build-up strip typically combine to overhang the base cabinets by 1½ in. Make right angle corner joints with mechanical fasteners (See step 1, page 91). Attach the subbase to the base cabinets with screws driven up through corner blocking or spreader rails in the base cabinets.

2 Cut pieces of 5⁄16 in. thick cementboard to fit on top of the subbase (cut cementboard by scoring with a utility knife then snapping along scored lines, as with wallboard). Apply a layer of thinset mortar to the plywood, then press the cementboard panels into place, making sure the edges are flush with the front and sides of the plywood. Drive 1 in. wallboard screws (four screws per square foot) through the cementboard and into the plywood. Cover seams with fiberglass mesh tape and thinset mortar.

3 Attach build-up strips to the front and side edges of the plywood subbase so the tops of the strips are flush with the surface of the cementboard. Use glue or panel adhesive and finish nails (or pneumatic pin nails) to attach the strips. If using a finished hardwood countertop edge treatment, install it now (See previous page).

4 Mark and cut the sink cutout and cutouts for other recessed countertop features, such as cooktops (See step 11, page 87). Make the cutout with a jig saw. Be sure to attach scrapwood supports to the top of the cutout after cutting partway through to prevent the waste from falling out early and ruining the cut.

5 Because the countertop subbase is square to begin with, there's no real need to spend a lot of time drawing layout and reference lines when laying a tile countertop. The best way to guarantee a good layout is to dry-lay the entire countertop before setting your first tile into the mortar. If you select an installation sequence that makes sense and do a good job of installing your first row, everything should fall in place just fine after that. The tile layout and installation sequences depend on, among other factors, the type of edge treatment you'll be using. As a general rule, you should start the layout by installing the tiles that are most critical to the edge treatment. On our tile countertop, that distinction was awarded to the horizontal, 3 × 12 in. bullnose tiles laid around the perimeter of the countertop. So we based our layout on the position of the bullnose edges of these tiles. To establish these positions, we first dry-laid a few field tiles in the corner area (here's another good general rule of layout: Start at the corners).

Then we laid a bullnose tile along the edge with the correct amount of overhang to cover the top of the vertical tile strip that would be attached to the countertop edge. With spacers between the bullnose tile and the field tiles, we used a combination square set at 45° to mark a miter-cutting line on the bullnose tile.

6 After miter-cutting the bullnose tile then cutting a mating bullnose tile at 45°, we dry-laid the border at the corner, allowing ¼ in. for a grout line at the miter joint. Then we used the positions of the bullnose tiles and field tiles as a guide for cutting our edge tile strips to length (first, however, we had field tiles cut to the proper width of 1¼ in.—the height of the build-up strip minus ¼ in. for a grout joint). The goal was to cut the edge tile so the grout lines between edge tiles would align with the grout lines between the field tiles, as well as the grout lines between bullnose tiles.

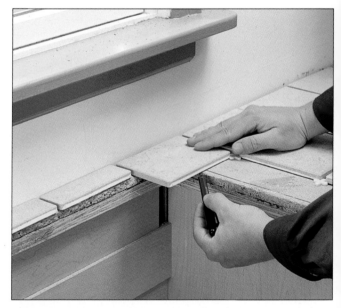

7 We dry-laid the rest of the field and border tiles, inserting plastic spacers between tiles as appropriate. If you need to trim the back row to fit (always trim the back row of tiles, not the front row), measure the trim size, allowing a ⅛ in. gap between the back edge of the back row and the wall. Around the sink cutout and at the ends of the runs, we marked field tiles for trimming to length.

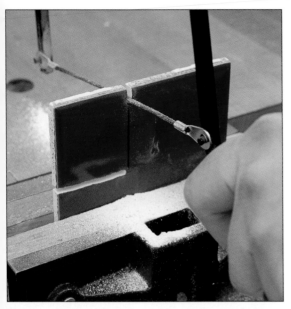

TIP: Cut all tiles to fit before you actually start laying tiles. For ceramic tiles, you can make straight cuts with a tile saw (See page 98) and internal cuts with a rod saw (above). But because the tiles for our project were porcelain (considerably harder than ceramic) we learned quickly that a tile cutter would not be efficient, so we rented a wet saw to make all the cuts.

8 Start setting the tiles, beginning with the edge tiles. To support the vertical edge tiles while the thinset mortar set up, we clamped a ledger beneath the build-up strip. The ledger also helps set the tiles at uniform height. Mix up a batch of thinset mortar, following the manufacturer's directions. If the mortar has no latex additive, add some to the mixture. Starting at an inside corner, "butter" the back of each tile with thinset and press it against the build-up strip. Insert plastic spacers between tiles (you'll need to remove them before laying the bullnose tiles).

9 Trowel thinset adhesive onto the sub-base with a square-notched trowel, then begin filling in the border and field tiles, fanning out from the inside corner. Set the border tiles so the front edges align with the faces of the edge tiles, and the grout lines align where possible.

10 Using spacers between tiles, install the rest of the field and border tiles. Work in small sections, and when each section is completed, seat the tiles by rapping lightly on the top edge of a 3 ft. long 2 × 4 wrapped in cloth or old carpet (this will help ensure that tiles are set to uniform depth).

11 After the countertop tiles have been laid and the thinset is set up, install the backsplash tiles. You can use narrow bullnose versions of the field tiles to make the backsplash, if they're available. We used the same 3 × 12 in. bullnose tiles that were used to make the borders. Attach the backsplash tiles by buttering the back sides with thinset mortar. Align the grout joints wherever possible.

12 Let the tiles set at least overnight, then grout the joints. Add latex reinforcement to the grout mixture, then mix with water to a syrupy but spreadable consistency. Pack grout into all joints, including vertical joints and mortar joints, using a grout float. Apply a coat of grout release agent to the surfaces of the tiles (inset photo) before grouting to make post-grout cleanup easier. NOTE: Grout is sold pretinted in a variety of colors—choose one that blends nicely with your tiles.

13 Sponge off any excess grout before it dries. Wipe diagonally with a dense sponge (a special grout sponge is shown above). Clean sponge after each pass. Wipe all the tiles once, then change the water and clean again, flipping the sponge to expose a fresh edge for each wipe.

14 Buff out grout residue with a soft cloth. For stubborn residue, dip the cloth in commercial grout and haze remover. After a few days, apply silicone grout sealer to the grout lines for extra protection. Install sink and other appliances (See pages 120 to 122).

Countertops
Solid surfacing countertops

Solid surfacing countertops are about as close as you can get to an ideal countertop surface. They are exceptionally durable, resist heat, are impenetrable to water, seldom stain and if they do get a scratch or a stain it can usually be sanded or buffed out. The material also can be machined with a router to create a number of decorative and functional effects, including drain boards, edge profiles and inset cutting boards. The material can also be custom formed into unusual shapes and sizes for island countertops, breakfast bars or just about any flat surface you can imagine. With a solid surfacing countertop you can mount a sink from below so water doesn't become trapped next to a rim. Or, you can have a sink made of the same material integrated seamlessly into the countertop surface. The only real drawbacks to these surfaces are the price and the fact that they should be built only by authorized installers. Still, if there is one area of your kitchen or bathroom remodeling project where you splurge a bit, solid surfacing countertops may be it. See page 83 for more discussion.

Integral sinks and profiled edges are just two of the features that have made solid surfacing countertops such a popular item in bathrooms as well as in kitchens.

Backsplashes made from solid surfacing material are chemically welded into grooves at the backs of solid surface countertops. The resulting backsplash effectively has no gaps that can trap water or germs.

Drain boards are one of the most overlooked features of a kitchen countertop, but for general hygiene they are hard to beat. Studies have shown that the cleanest way to dry dishes is to let them air dry in a well-drained area. Tapered grooves routed into the surface of a solid surface countertop channel water runoff safely into the sink. A special jig is used to guide the router bit so it cuts grooves that start out shallow and deepen as they near the sink, so the surface of the countertop is not affected.

A traditional countertop material for centuries in some parts of the world, concrete is enjoying a new popularity as a counter surface in kitchens and bathrooms here in the United States.

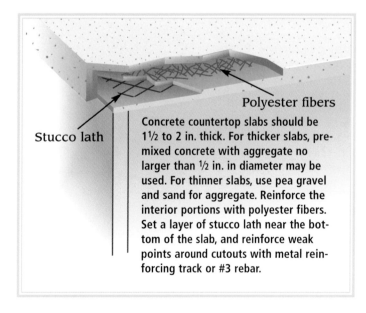

Stucco lath

Polyester fibers

Concrete countertop slabs should be 1½ to 2 in. thick. For thicker slabs, pre-mixed concrete with aggregate no larger than ½ in. in diameter may be used. For thinner slabs, use pea gravel and sand for aggregate. Reinforce the interior portions with polyester fibers. Set a layer of stucco lath near the bottom of the slab, and reinforce weak points around cutouts with metal reinforcing track or #3 rebar.

Countertops
Poured concrete

Concrete is one of the most important building materials in use today. We see it all around us, in roads, sidewalks, foundations, swimming pools, driveways and even garden furnishings and decorations. It offers superior durability and it can be molded into just about any shape that's needed. And on top of that, it is cheap. So why does the idea of using concrete to build a countertop strike us as so strange? In fact, for centuries many cultures have relied upon the low cost and workability of concrete for exactly that purpose. And today, here in this country, we're finally starting to catch on. But where the countertops you'll see fashioned from concrete in less prosperous parts of the world tend to resemble county highways shrunk down and dropped on top of a plain but sturdy masonry base, the American version is more sophisticated.

Creative designers and tradesmen have discovered that with some innovative finishing work, poured concrete doesn't need to look like a driveway.

In this chapter you'll see a clear case study that shows how easy it is to fashion your own countertop with ordinary concrete. The stunning black island countertop featured is made from only three bags of basic concrete mix, with a few special ingredients thrown in to increase strength and give it the rich colors and smooth surface we desire in our kitchens and baths. If you have a little patience, a sense of adventure and some experience working with concrete, you've already got all the tools you need.

With concrete, as with any countertop material, you need to make a few choices up front. There are a number of finishing options that create vastly different appearances, from the raw industrial look of plain cement to the elegant, monolithic feel of imported marble and granite. The photo to the right illustrates just a few of the possibilities. And there are practical considerations. Should the countertop be cast in place or formed off-site then attached to your cabinets after it is finished? If, like most people, you're using the medium for indoor purposes for the first time, the best advice is to start small and see how it goes. A small island countertop like the one shown in this section is far easier to cast than a large countertop with a backsplash and multiple cutouts for sinks and appliances.

You'll also need to make some choices about mixing ratios and reinforcement. If you respond to a natural concrete color, or one close to it (like the charcoal-colored countertop shown here), you can use bagged, premixed concrete as the basic ingredient. But if you'd prefer a lighter or a very dark color, you'll need to mix your concrete from scratch using white Portland cement. If this is the direction you're interested in going, you'll need to get some additional information on mixing ratios for concrete. Here's a tip, though: For best results use a concrete mixing ratio that's very rich (it has a higher-than-normal proportion of white Portland cement).

To help make your choice, try casting a few samples with different colors and different finishes. The brief instructions accompanying each of the samples to the right will give you enough information to get started and to experiment. And when you're done, at the very least you will have created a few interesting stepping stones for your garden, or perhaps even a top for a small indoor/outdoor planter. More than anything else, be creative and be prepared to have some fun.

Recipes for concrete finishes

Solid tone finishes (A, C, E): Mix white Portland cement, pea gravel, latex additive, concrete pigment and water. For a gray or charcoal colored finish you can use premixed concrete bags, as we do in the project demonstrated in this chapter. For light to medium colors, you can use liquid concrete pigment like you'll see used here. For very dark finishes, you'll have better success with dry stucco pigment.

Marble or travertine finishes (B, D): To achieve a countertop that has a look and feel reminiscent of expensive imported marble, use two or three different colors of concrete. The samples shown here were made by pressing together clumps of light and dark concrete into the concrete form. You'll still need to float the concrete surface, though, which tends to blend the colors together. So you'll get best results by casting the countertop upside down. When you release the forms, use a third color as a skiff coat (See step 13, page 112) to fill in small pock marks or crevices in the surface of the countertop.

Tools & materials for building concrete countertops

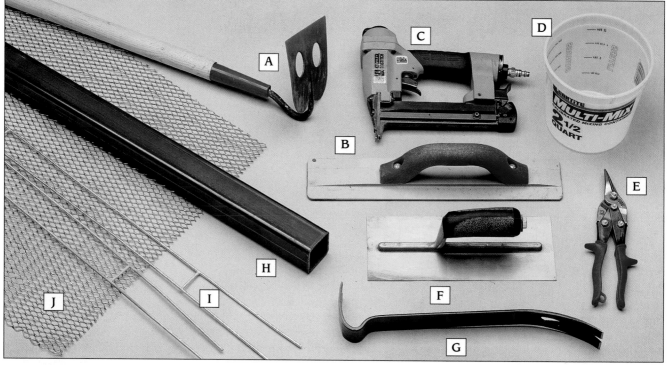

Special tools and reinforcing products you'll need for building concrete countertop forms and pouring concrete countertops include: masonry hoe for working mixture in mortar tub or wheelbarrow (A); steel float for packing mixture into form (B); pneumatic stapler for building forms (optional) (C); calibrated mixing vessel for blending liquid ingredients (D); aviator snips for cutting metal reinforcement (E); steel trowel for finishing surface (F); pry bar for releasing forms (G); 2 × 2 square metal tube 18 in. longer than widest part of form for striking off surface (H); metal reinforcement tracks or #3 rebar (I); stucco lath (J); and concrete ingredients (see below).

Mixing concrete for countertops

The appearance and longevity of your concrete countertop depend greatly on the precision and thoroughness with which the concrete mixture is prepared. The basic strategy is to blend the dry ingredients. For the project shown here, 60# bags of premixed concrete mix, Portland cement and polyester fibers (lower, interior section only) are the dry ingredients. Then, mix the liquid ingredients in a calibrated mixing vessel, taking careful notes of the amounts included for each batch. Liquid ingredients for this project included: water, latex concrete additive and liquid concrete dye. Mix one bag at a time, measuring ingredients carefully.

1 (For concrete used in project that follows) Start by emptying one 60# bag of premixed concrete into a mortar tub or wheelbarrow. Blend in two quarts of white Portland cement. For midsection (See step 4, page 109) add polyester fibers to the dry mixture. Work with a masonry hoe.

2 Mix liquid ingredients in measured amounts from a calibrated mixing vessel. Start with two gallons of water. Add latex fortifier in proportions directed on container. Add liquid pigment (optional)—we used two ounces of charcoal pigment per gallon of water. Blend and add to dry ingredients. Add more water as needed, keeping careful track of amounts. Work with a masonry hoe to dry consistency (See step 2, page 109).

How to make a cast-in-place concrete countertop form

Casting your concrete countertop in place has two principal advantages: you don't have to transport the finished counter-top, which will weigh close to 20 pounds per square foot; and for larger projects, you can make the countertop seamless. On the downside, you'll make quite a mess in your kitchen or bathroom, and you should only use sealers that do not require etching of the surface with a muriatic acid solution. Building a form is also much trickier for a cast-in-place slab, especially if you want to include a breakfast bar overhang as shown here. If you plan to install a sink or cooktop, a precast form with blockouts is a better way to go (See next page).

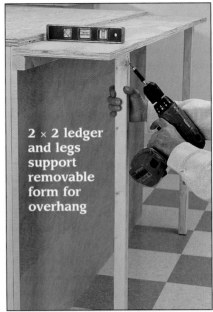

2 × 2 ledger and legs support removable form for overhang

1 Measure the exact outside dimensions of the cabinet or cabinets that will support the concrete countertop. Cut a plywood substrate to exactly this dimension from ³⁄₄ in. thick exterior grade plywood. If you plan to cast a countertop with a significant overhang, as in the island breakfast bar we planned for the cabinet bases above, add the width of the overhang, minus 1¹⁄₂ in., and cut your substrate. Attach the substrate to the cabinets with 2 in. deck screws.

OPTION: If you're casting an overhanging breakfast bar, one way to create a remov-able form base for the overhang is to cut a plywood base the exact size of the overhang and support it in position from below so the top is even with the bottom of the main form base.

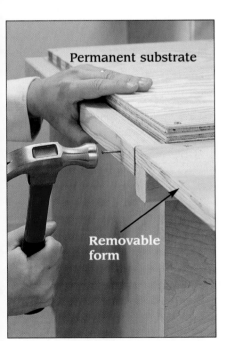

Permanent substrate

Removable form

2 Cut 2 × 2 spacers and attach them to the cabinets so the tops of the spacers are flush with the bottom of the perma-nent substrate. The spacers should fully encircle the substrate and be flush with the outside edges of the removable ply-wood form. Tack them to the cabinets with 8d finish nails.

3 Cut side forms equal in width to the sum of the spacers (1¹⁄₂ in.), the sub-base (³⁄₄ in.) and the thickness of the countertop (1¹⁄₂ in.). Attach the forms by driving 3 in. deck screws through the sides and into the edges of the form base. Also lock-screw the form boards at the corners. The tops should be level.

4 Coat the inside surfaces of the form boards with vegetable oil to prevent water from leeching out of the concrete and into the plywood. The oil also makes the side form boards and overhang base easier to strip off.

How to make a precast concrete countertop form

Precasting your concrete countertop in a location away from the installation area keeps the mess out of your kitchen or bathroom, and is, in most regards, a much easier forming task. The finished concrete slab is simply removed from the forms and set directly onto the cabinets. Working outdoors or in a garage also allows you to properly etch and rinse the cured slab, opening up a number of options for treating and sealing the surface. But if

the countertop you're making is larger than about 15 square feet, you'll probably need to cast it in two pieces then join the sections together on-site. The best way to join sections is to cast correctly aligned mortises for mechanical fasteners into each section so you can draw the sections together on top of the cabinets. But this will create a visible seam. Blockouts for sinks and other cutouts are attached to the form, then cut out.

1 Make blockouts for cutouts in the countertop. In the project shown here, a bar sink requiring a 14¼ in. square cutout was needed. For maximum strength and resistance to chipping, the corners of the cutout should be rounded. We made a blockout from a double layer of ¾ in. exterior plywood, using the sink cutout template as a guide. We gang-cut the parts on the band saw, then gang-sanded the corners smooth. To make it easier to release the form after the concrete cured, we cut out the center of the blockout. Then, we laid the blockout on top of a piece of melamine board (used for the form base) and measured the total thickness so we'd know exactly how wide to make the sides of the form.

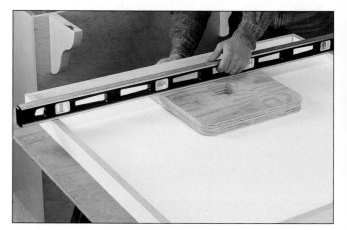

2 Cut a form base the same dimensions as the planned countertop, using ¾ in. thick melamine particle board. Rip side form strips from ¾ in. melamine board (the strips should be the same width as the thickness measured in step 1, and sized to wrap around all four sides of the form base). Set the side forms in position next to the base, then set the blockout in position on the top (melamine coated) face of the base. Lay a straightedge across the curb and two opposite sides to make sure the tops of all parts are aligned. If the sides are higher than the curb, you'll need to trim them down to fit on the table saw. If the curb is higher, adjust the sides upward and clamp them in exact position with bar clamps.

3 If you own an air-driven stapler, attach the sides of the form with 1½ in. crown staples driven through the sides and into the edges of the base at 5 to 6 in. intervals. If you don't have an air stapler, use 1½ in. wallboard screws (but be aware that they may break when you try to break down the form after the countertop is cast). Make sure the tops of the form sides are exactly flush with the top of the blockout.

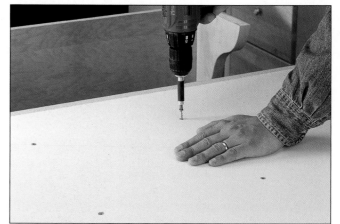

4 Tape the blockout securely in position, then flip the form upside down and attach the blockout with 1½ in. deck screws driven up through the base and into the blockout (drill countersunk pilot holes first). Because the form surfaces that contact the concrete are melamine-coated, you do not need to oil the forms. Recheck with a straightedge to make sure form sides and blockout align.

How to make a concrete countertop

1 Make your form—either precast (See previous page) or cast in place (See page 107). Plan out the sizes and quantities of stucco lath and rebar or reinforcing track you'll need. Reinforcement should be inserted around cutouts, and about 1 in. back from the front edge on larger countertops. Cut the lath and rebar before you start mixing and placing the concrete. TIP: Use tape to mark cutouts in stucco lath and cut with aviator snips.

2 Mix a small batch of concrete (See page 106) WITHOUT polyester fiber reinforcement. Be sure to make a note of the amounts of water and pigment (if any) you add so future batches can be mixed to the same color and consistency. For countertops, concrete should be a drier consistency than for other concrete projects: just damp enough so it doesn't crumble apart when squeezed into a ball.

3 Pack the unreinforced concrete around the edges of the form. The concrete should be packed so it's about a couple of inches thick at the edges and it fills all the way to the tops of the form sides. Pound vigorously on the concrete to make sure it completely fills the area and is well-packed.

4 Mix a batch of concrete WITH polyester fiber reinforcement and press it into the bottom of the form to a depth of about 1 in. Lay stucco lath inside the form area. The lath should be no closer than 1 in. to any edge or blockout. Lay strips of metal track reinforcement or #3 (3/8 in.) rebar on top of the fresh concrete, about 1 to 2 in. in from the edges of the blockout.

How to make a concrete countertop (cont.)

5 Working quickly, mix another batch of concrete WITHOUT fiber reinforcement and shovel it on top of the stucco lath until the level reaches slightly higher than the tops of the forms. Press the concrete down vigorously so all voids are filled and well-packed. NOTE: Polyester fiber reinforcement adds a significant amount of strength to concrete and therefore is a useful addition to the "foundation" of the slab. But the whisker-like fibers will protrude through the surface if used near edges or the slab top, and you will never be able to get a smooth surface. That's why it's important to make sure the fibers are left out of these areas completely.

6 Tamp the concrete with a magnesium float to pack it tightly into the form, then float the surface with the float until smooth. This step is where the most "sweat equity" is required. Add small amounts of concrete as needed to fill in any low spots. If any larger pieces of aggregate work their way to the surface, remove them and fill in blemishes with fresh concrete. Continue adding concrete until the surface is smooth, well-packed and slightly crowned.

7 Strike off the concrete. This is a very important step in the process and is best accomplished with a helper. A 2 in. square metal bar at least 18 in. longer than the form width is the best tool for the job. Scrape the bar back and forth to level and smooth the surface. The leading edge of the bar should be upturned slightly with each pass so it doesn't catch on the concrete (you'll understand why you want to avoid this once you start). Continue striking off the surface until it is exactly level with the tops of the form sides and the blockout, and the surface is smooth and slick.

8 Let the concrete set up for 1 to 1½ hours, then float the surface with a steel trowel. Take care not to overwork the concrete: this can draw aggregate too close to the surface, causing pop-outs and weakening the countertop. If you are working in hot or dry conditions, cover the concrete with plastic or wet burlap as it cures. Let the concrete cure for at least 48 hours.

9 Release the concrete forms by prying carefully between the inside edges of the forms and the concrete with a flat pry bar. Unscrew the blockout from below (but you probably won't be able to remove it right away—that's okay). Wait until you've actually installed the countertop, as the presence of the blockout helps prevent the slab from cracking when it is moved.

10 Ease sharp edges and corners by sanding with a random-orbit sander and 100-grit sandpaper. For a more streamlined look, you may wait to shape bevels into the corners and edges with a disc grinder and masonry wheel (but be forewarned that this will create a substantial amount of dust and mess).

11 Etch the surfaces and edges of the countertop with a very diluted muriatic solution. On countertops made with pigmented concrete, an acid wash exposes more of the color and texture variations for a more decorative look. An acid wash should only be used on countertops that are precast and can be removed to a well-ventilated and easy-to-clean work area. Follow the manufacturer's instructions for diluting and applying the muriatic acid solution, but be sure to make it very weak—no more than one ounce of acid per gallon of water.

12 Rinse the countertop slab thoroughly with water to neutralize the acid, then let it air dry.

13 Prepare a stiff, peanut-buttery mixture of Portland cement, latex fortifier and liquid pigment and coat the the surfaces and exposed edges with it. Scrape (or "skiff") the surface and edges with a grout float to remove the mixture from the even surfaces (it will fill in any pock marks or other small cracks for a more even appearance). Let the mixture cure for an hour. NOTE: This is an optional step, but is a very good idea if you want to have a smooth, rich surface. After the surface dries, sand it with an orbital sander and 180-grit sanding discs until the desired smoothness is reached (plan on going through a lot of discs!).

14 Apply a heavy bead of construction adhesive or silicone caulk to the the tops of the base cabinets that will support the countertop.

15 Get plenty of help for transporting the countertop to the installation area: not only is handling the countertop with too few people dangerous, it also creates stresses that can lead to cracks or structural failure. Set the countertop on the cabinets so the side overhangs are equal. No additional fasteners are needed.

16 Remove the blockout by cutting from the interior cutout toward the countertop. Avoid contacting the concrete (but don't get too worried about it, since the sink or cooktop flange will cover the edge of the cutout).

17 Seal concrete with acrylic concrete sealing product. Apply the sealer according to the manufacturer's directions. If you will be preparing food on the surface, be sure to use a nontoxic sealer. Buff out the final coat of sealant to the desired gloss, using an artificial wool scrubbing pad. For larger surfaces or to achieve a very high gloss, attach a soft buffing wheel to your electric drill. Install sink, cooktop or other cutout appliances (See pages 120 to 122).

NOTE: If you've cast your countertop in place, you'll need to conceal the exposed edges of the plywood substrate by adding an extension to the cabinet face frame or by applying matching veneer edge tape.

Plumbing fixtures

This chapter provides information about choosing and installing the types of plumbing fixtures that are dealt with most frequently in kitchen and bathroom remodeling: sinks, faucets, toilets, bathtubs and showers. The types of projects featured here would not be considered "major" plumbing projects by most people: they are relatively simple installations that anyone with some basic do-it-yourself skills (and, in some cases, a good set of instructions from the manufacturer) can accomplish.

We've also included some very basic information on home plumbing and handling plumbing materials. But it would not be reasonable to think you can attack a major project (adding drain lines or plumbing an addition, for example) without a considerable amount of specific information and advice from other sources. The best place to start is always with your local building inspectors.

Plumbing codes

Because of the potential for disastrous water damage and the high cost of repairing a plumbing system once it's up and running, plumbing is a closely regulated practice. The Uniform Plumbing Code (UPC) is a national set of codes that's updated every three years. It forms the foundation of most local plumbing codes. But for a number of reasons, including climate, local codes often vary from the UPC standards—usually on the more restrictive side. Use the UPC as a general guide when planning a plumbing project or repair, but make sure to consult with your local building inspection department before beginning any major work. For new installations, a permit is normally required.

Sinks and faucets can contribute significantly to the design scheme of a bathroom or kitchen, as the undermount sink attached beneath this solid surfacing countertop demonstrates. Avoid skimping on faucets. The few extra dollars you'll pay up front for a good one more than offset the grief that can be caused by a perpetually leaking faucet.

The sink is the hub of a whole system of fixtures and appliances in today's kitchens. In most cases, the plumbing that supplies water and carries away waste for the sink also supports a dishwasher and garbage disposer, and perhaps even a water purification system or ice maker.

You don't always need to buy expensive, top of the line fixtures to achieve pleasing design results. This relatively inexpensive five-piece tileboard tub surround kit works with the rich wall colors to make a high-contrast, dynamic shower area.

Shower stalls and tub surround doors offer a unique opportunity to bring interesting new textures into a bathroom. Here, a glass surround adds a sense of sweeping motion and even a little warmth to a chiseled, ultra-modern bathroom.

Pedestal sinks are enjoying a surge in popularity. In addition to the more contemporary model shown above, replicas of elegant pedestal sinks from the Art Deco period also are in favor with designers.

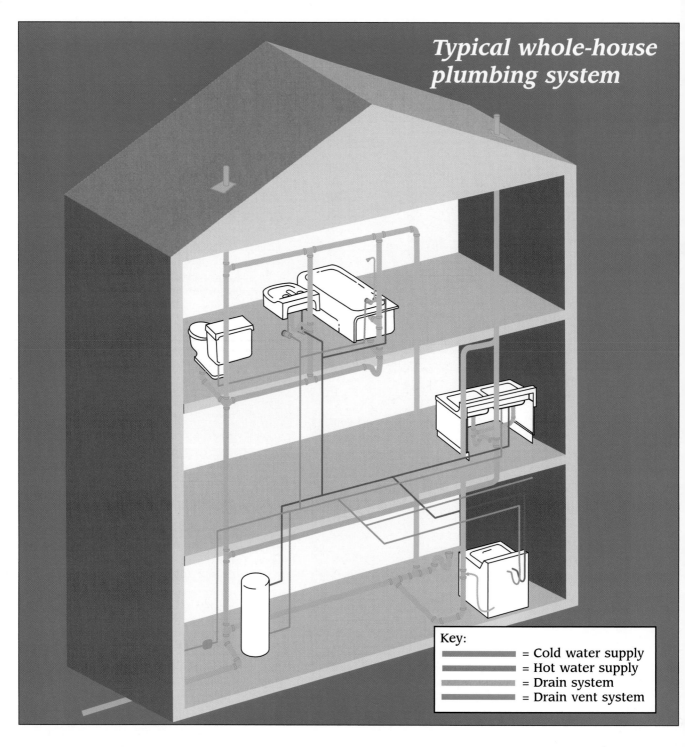

Typical whole-house plumbing system

Key:
- = Cold water supply
- = Hot water supply
- = Drain system
- = Drain vent system

Home plumbing systems

The sinks, tubs, showers and toilets in our homes are only the business ends of a comprehensive network of supply, waste and vent pipes. Modern fixtures and hook-up products made especially for the do-it-yourselfer can be installed by people with very little experience with (or even knowledge of) plumbing systems. But major plumbing projects, such as adding branch water supply lines or moving drain pipes, should be left to professionals or at least very experienced do-it-yourselfers.

But even if you're hiring out the work, it doesn't hurt to have a basic understanding of how a plumbing system works. In essence, clean water enters your house under pressure through the water main. Supply pipes carry water from the main to the water heater. From there, hot and cold water are directed throughout your home in pairs of supply tubes. Waste water is conveyed from the various drains in your home to a main drain stack via branch drain lines. Each fixture and each drain line must also be vented to prevent pressure build-up in the system that could cause back-ups.

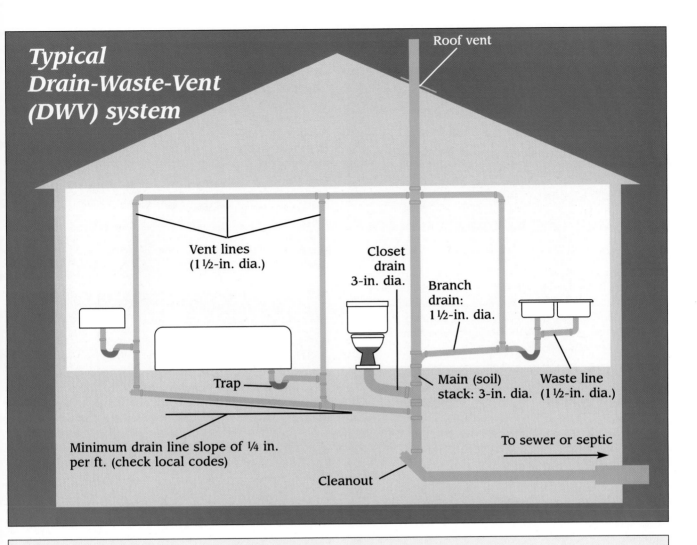

Typical Drain-Waste-Vent (DWV) system

Roof vent

Vent lines (1½-in. dia.)

Closet drain 3-in. dia.

Branch drain: 1½-in. dia.

Trap

Main (soil) stack: 3-in. dia.

Waste line (1½-in. dia.)

Minimum drain line slope of ¼ in. per ft. (check local codes)

To sewer or septic

Cleanout

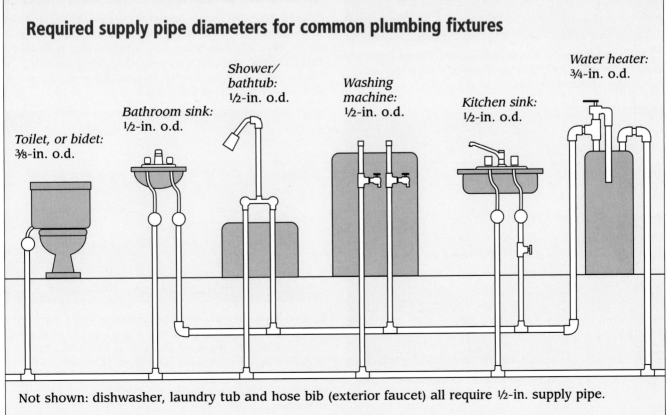

Required supply pipe diameters for common plumbing fixtures

Water heater: ¾-in. o.d.

Shower/bathtub: ½-in. o.d.

Washing machine: ½-in. o.d.

Bathroom sink: ½-in. o.d.

Kitchen sink: ½-in. o.d.

Toilet, or bidet: ⅜-in. o.d.

Not shown: dishwasher, laundry tub and hose bib (exterior faucet) all require ½-in. supply pipe.

How to solvent weld plastic pipe

1 Cut the pipe with a hack saw or power miter saw, then deburr with a utility knife. Sand the outside of the pipe and the inside of the connection hub using sandcloth or emery paper before applying primer.

Materials used to solvent-weld PVC pipe include colored solvent and primer labeled for use with PVC pipe, and sandcloth or emery paper for smoothing rough edges. Primer helps degloss the pipe's slick surface, ensuring a good seal. Solvents and primers are toxic and flammable. Provide good ventilation and keep these products away from heat.

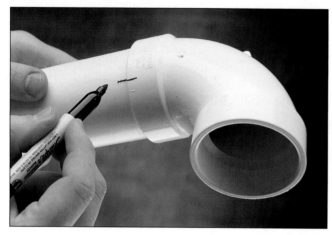

2 Wipe the pipes clean then fit the pipes and fittings together in the desired layout. Draw an alignment mark across each joint with a permanent marker.

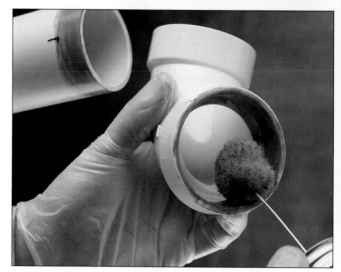

3 Apply PVC primer to the outside of the pipe and the inside of the connection hub or fitting. The primer is colored so you can see when full coverage has been achieved. Wear disposable gloves, and make sure the work area is adequately ventilated. Also be sure to read the directions and safety precautions on the labels of all products you'll be using.

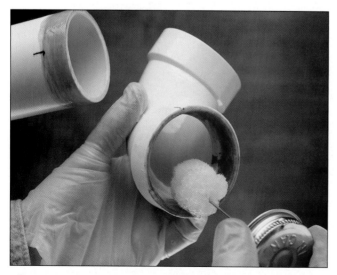

4 Apply a thick coat of solvent glue to the outside of the pipe and a thin coat on the inside of the connection hub.

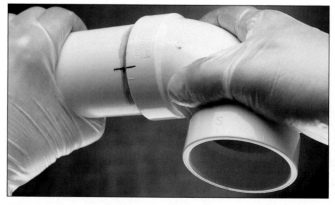

5 Quickly slip the pipes and fittings together so the alignment mark you drew across the joint is about 2 in. off center, then twist the pipes into alignment. This will ensure the solvent is spread evenly. The solvent will set in about 30 seconds, so don't waste time. Hold the pipes steady for another 20 seconds, then wipe away excess solvent with a rag. Don't disturb the joint for 30 minutes.

How to install a shutoff valve

It's a rare kitchen or bathroom remodeling project that won't require you to install at least one new shutoff valve. According to the Uniform Plumbing Code, every water supply line leading into a plumbing fixture should have a working shutoff valve. That way, if you're repairing a toilet, for example, you can turn off the water supply without affecting the rest of the house. And if a fixture should spring a leak, you can turn off the water immediately. Here you'll see how to attach a shutoff valve featuring a compression fitting to a fixture supply tube.

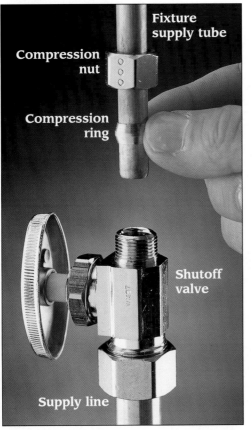

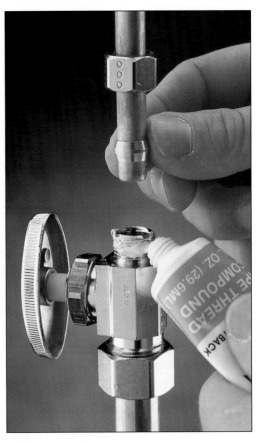

1 Solder the shutoff valve to the incoming supply line, then cut the fixture supply tube to length, allowing ½ in. for the portion that will fit inside the shutoff valve. Slip a compression ring and compression nut (usually included with valve) onto the end of the fixture supply pipe.

2 Apply pipe joint compound to the threads of the valve opening. The compound will serve as a lubricant during compression.

3 Insert the fixture supply tube into the valve and hand-tighten the compression nut over the compression ring.

4 Tighten the compression nut with two wrenches. Turn on the water supply. If the fitting leaks, try gently tightening the nuts.

Installing sinks & faucets

The vast majority of kitchen and bathroom sinks installed today are self-rimming, drop-in style fixtures. Lighter weight sinks (such as stainless steel kitchen sinks) are attached to the countertop with clips that hold them in place. Heavier sinks, like cast-iron kitchen sinks, rely mainly on their own weight and the stabilizing effect of the plumbing connected to them to stay put. A bead of adhesive caulk between the rim of the sink and the countertop helps a little, but its primary purpose is to block water from seeping under the rim. If you're installing a new sink, attach the faucet body to the sink before you mount the sink.

Once the sink is in place, hook up the drain by attaching the drain body to the sink basin, then using the P-trap assembly to transition from the drain tailpiece to the drain arm extending from the wall. The P-trap, trap arm and drain tailpiece normally are purchased as a kit. The tailpiece and trap arm are cut to length to fit your drain configuration. Connections are made with slip washers and slip nuts. In kitchen sink drains, the process is complicated slightly by the facts that kitchen sinks typically have two bowls with separate drains, and a dishwasher and garbage disposer usually drain through the system as well (See page 122). Make sure to buy a drain kit that is correct for your sink situation.

After the drain is hooked up, connect the faucet to the water supply at the shutoff valves. This connection is made with flexible tubing. The tubing is sold in many different lengths with a threaded coupling of varying diameters at each end. Check to see which sizes you'll need by measuring the outside diameters of the faucet tailpieces and the nipples at the shutoff valves.

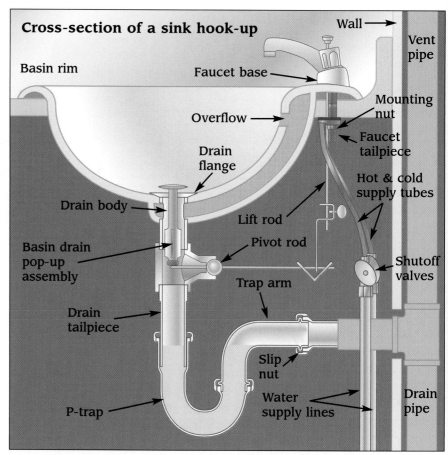

Cross-section of a sink hook-up

Wall — Vent pipe — Basin rim — Faucet base — Overflow — Mounting nut — Drain flange — Faucet tailpiece — Drain body — Hot & cold supply tubes — Lift rod — Basin drain pop-up assembly — Pivot rod — Shutoff valves — Trap arm — Drain tailpiece — Slip nut — Water supply lines — Drain pipe — P-trap

Plumbing is very similar for bathroom and kitchen sinks. The main difference is in the way the drain bodies are assembled and the absence of a pop-up drain closer in kitchen sinks. Also, kitchen sink drain and supply systems frequently are connected to dishwashers, garbage disposers and other appliances (See page 122).

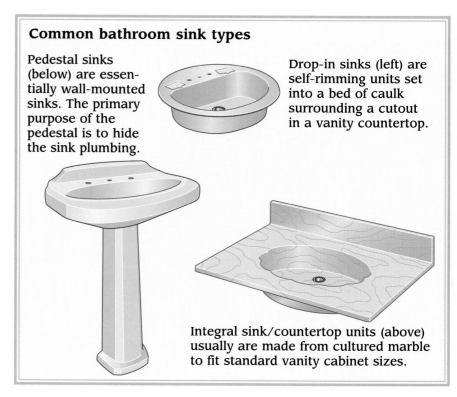

Common bathroom sink types

Pedestal sinks (below) are essentially wall-mounted sinks. The primary purpose of the pedestal is to hide the sink plumbing.

Drop-in sinks (left) are self-rimming units set into a bed of caulk surrounding a cutout in a vanity countertop.

Integral sink/countertop units (above) usually are made from cultured marble to fit standard vanity cabinet sizes.

How to hook up bathroom sink plumbing

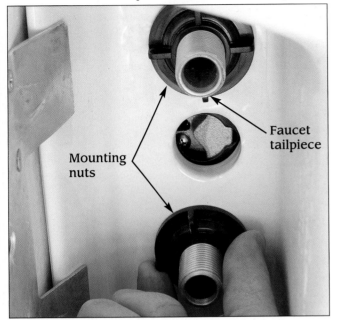

Mounting nuts

Faucet tailpiece

1 Mount the sink to the wall or the vanity cabinet. Lay rings of plumber's putty around the water supply holes in the faucet mounting area of the sink. Seat the faucet in place with the tailpieces extending through the correct holes. From below, thread mounting nuts onto the tailpieces and tighten. In most cases, hand-tightening is sufficient to secure the faucet, but if you are unable to access the nuts well enough to apply significant hand-torque, use a basin wrench to tighten the nuts. But be very careful not to overtighten the nuts.

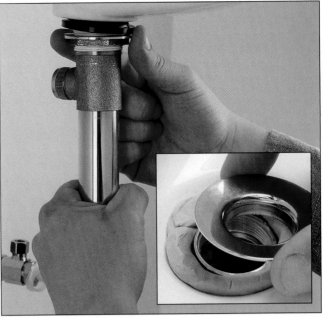

2 Apply a coil of plumber's putty beneath the drain flange and press the flange into the drain opening (inset photo). Wrap the threaded drain body fitting with teflon tape. Then assemble the parts of the drain body and the tailpiece, and connect them to the flange by tightening the mounting nuts. The opening for the pivot rod should face straight back toward the center of the faucet body. Attach the drain arm to the drain stubout if necessary, then attach the P-trap to the arm and the tailpiece.

3 Insert the ball-end of the pivot rod into the pivot rod opening and tighten the nut that secures the rod to the drain. Connect the lift rod from the faucet to the pivot rod using the pivot rod strap. Adjust the strap so the pivot rod is horizontal when the pop-up is open.

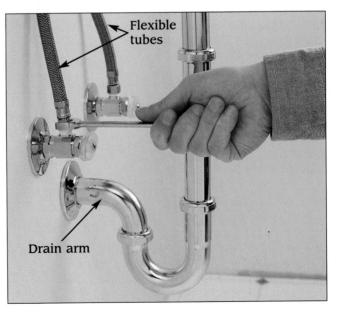

Flexible tubes

Drain arm

4 Hook flexible supply tubes up to the tailpieces. Typically, the supply tubes attach with threaded compression fittings. With the shutoff valve at the water supply lines closed, attach the tubes to the shutoff. Double-check to make sure you're connecting hot to hot and cold to cold. NOTE: The tailpieces and the nipples on the shutoffs often will be different sizes. Be sure to check both before purchasing supply tubes. In some cases, you may need to use an adapter at one end. Open shutoff valves.

Drain connections for sink, dishwasher & garbage disposer

Kitchen sinks, dishwashers and garbage disposers normally share a drain system that routes through the sink drain. The dishwasher drains waste through a flexible tube that feeds into the disposer. To prevent water from backing up into the dishwasher, the drain hose should be routed through an air gap. The air gap is a simple device that mounts to the sink, usually through the hole for the sprayer hose (unless you have a four-hole sink). It has two nipples beneath the sink and the open top is protected by a decorative cylindrical cap.

The disposer drains through a discharge tube into a continuous waste pipe that connects with a T-fitting into the drain tailpiece from the sink.

Begin by installing the disposer. Disposers are suspended from the sink with a series of mounting rings that are drawn together with screws. Once the disposer is set, attach the upturned end of a continuous waste pipe to the discharge tube with a slip nut and washer. Then, adjust the location of the drain tailpiece and T-fitting so the opening in the T-fitting is aligned with the continuous waste pipe. You may need to remove the waste pipe and cut it to length. Then, assemble the drain lines with slip nuts and washers. Finally, attach the drain hose from the dishwasher to the higher nipple on the air gap. Then attach a hose from the lower nipple to the nipple on the disposer. Use hose clamps to secure the connections. Make sure the drain hoses are free of kinks or sharp curves.

NOTE: Hot water for the dishwasher is provided by connecting a flexible supply tube from a two-outlet shutoff valve at the hot water supply tube for the sink faucet. Check your local codes before making wiring connections: many codes require that the dishwasher and disposer be on separate electrical circuits (but they can still share an electrical box). Follow all manufacturer's directions for installing disposer and dishwasher.

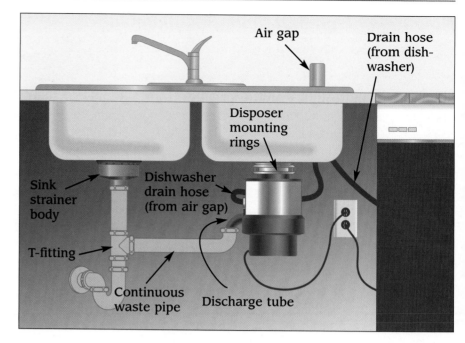

Air gap

Drain hose (from dishwasher)

Disposer mounting rings

Sink strainer body

Dishwasher drain hose (from air gap)

T-fitting

Continuous waste pipe

Discharge tube

Specialty tools for installing sinks & faucets

(A): A spud wrench is equipped with hooked jaws that latch onto the lugs on sink drain mounting nuts.

(B): A basin wrench is used to remove or tighten hard-to-reach mounting nuts that thread onto faucet tailpieces.

(C): Allen wrenches fit into allen areas that secure a faucet spout to a faucet body.

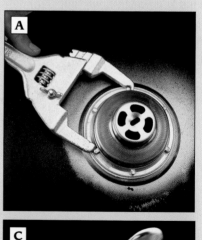

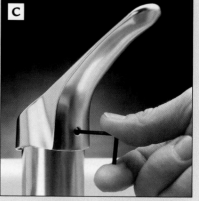

Installing bathtub & shower fixtures

Installing bathtubs and showers has gotten much easier over the years. It wasn't too long ago that any shower required a custom-poured mortar base with metal reinforcement. Drains were fashioned from oakum and other hard-to-handle materials. Today, the availability of do-it-yourselfer friendly kits has greatly simplified the process. And new advances in plastics and polymers have brought us newer, lightweight alternatives to traditional cast iron and porcelain. Bathtubs, for example, are now made from polymers that have many of the same properties of much heavier materials, as well as plastic, fiberglass, and lightweight pressed steel.

Shower and tub surrounds are almost always installed as kits these days, compared to the clunky, site-built efforts that always seemed to leak or lose their surfacing. Along with these advances, some new accessories have been developed, including prefabricated glass doors that are a breeze to mount.

But one outcome of the flood of new products in this area is that every product you buy seems to have slightly different installation methods. Standardization has become a thing of the past. In the sequences contained in this section, we show you some examples of how these new materials and kits are installed. But as likely as not, the unit you buy won't be installed in exactly the same way. Nevertheless, we've tried to select fairly representative products to work with and to present them in a way that emphasizes the general ideas over the specific details. When combined with the manufacturer's instructions that came with your product, you should have all the information you need.

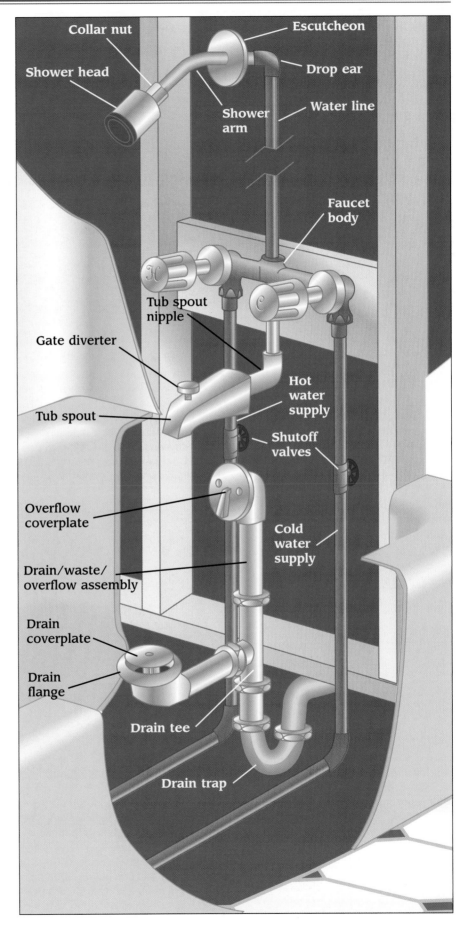

Collar nut — Escutcheon — Shower head — Drop ear — Shower arm — Water line — Faucet body — Tub spout nipple — Gate diverter — Hot water supply — Tub spout — Shutoff valves — Overflow coverplate — Cold water supply — Drain/waste/overflow assembly — Drain coverplate — Drain flange — Drain tee — Drain trap

How to install an alcove bathtub

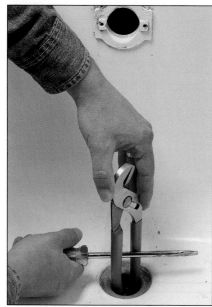

1 Close the shutoff valve and begin to remove the old tub. Start by taking off the faucet handles and escutcheons, overflow coverplate, the tub spout and the shower head, arm and escutcheon. To remove the drain assembly, first take out the plug then twist off the drain flange assembly. You can remove the drain flange assembly by inserting the handles of pliers in through the top and twisting the handles counterclockwise with a screwdriver.

2 Cut back or remove the wallcovering around the top of the tub to expose the vertical tub nailing flanges. Depending on the type of surround you'll be installing and the condition of the old wallcoverings, you may want to completely remove the wallcovering. Because our plan was to build a custom tile surround (which requires cement-board backer boards) we removed the wallboard completely in the tub area. If you're installing tileboard or a kit-style surround with thin panels, remove just a few inches of the wallcovering above the tub, then patch in with new material after the new tub is installed. Before removing the wallboard we scored vertical lines up to the ceiling above the outer corners of the tub. We used a flat pry bar to pull off the wallboard.

3 Pry out any nails or screws that are fastening the tub to the wall along the vertical nailing flange. Also cut any caulking seals at the base of tub apron with a utility knife.

4 From the access panel located on the opposite side of the wall, unscrew the slip nut attaching the drain tailpiece onto the drain pipe in the floor. Slide the old tub out of the tub area, then stuff a rag in the drain pipe. Because many alcove-style tubs are installed into a mortar bed, you may need to rock the tub back and forth to break it free from the mortar. A couple of 1 × 4s laid flat can be used for skids to make the tub easier to slide and provide clearance for any drain assembly parts still attached to the tub. Dispose of the old tub immediately. Heavy cast-iron tubs can be cut into smaller pieces using a reciprocating saw with a metal-cutting blade.

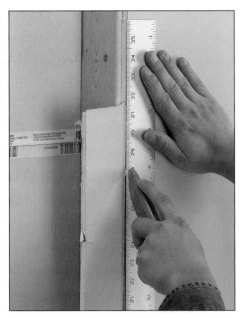

Cross-braces

Old ledger

5 Inspect the subfloor for damage. If you find a suspicious area, remove a small section of the subfloor and test the floor joists below by probing with a screwdriver. If joists are compromised, consult a building inspector. Locate the next wall stud outside the tub area on each side and score vertical cutting lines centered on the wall studs, then remove wallboard up to the lines.

6 If adding a shower, install new supply pipes and fittings now. You'll need to replace the faucet with one containing a diverter valve and add a supply tube that extends up from the diverter valve to the shower head height (usually, about 72 in. above the floor). Both the faucet body and the elbow for the shower arm and head should be mounted to crossbraces in the stud cavity. Set the new tub in place to see how it fits. We found that our tub was slightly narrower and shorter than the old one, so we removed the old ledger and ripped thin strips of 2 × 4 to fur out the wall studs so the drain opening on the tub would be lined up with the drain pipe, as seen in the next photo.

Furring strips

New ledger

7 Attach the new ledger so the top of the 2 × 4 is at the height of the bottom of the tub rim. Keep the ledger clear of the ends of the tub area by a few inches.

8 Slide the new tub into the installation area so you can check the fit. Make sure it rests flush on the ledger (or above it by no more than ¼ in.). Also check to make sure the drain opening is located over the drain pipe. Because our project included building a partition wall at the foot of the tub, we also marked the location for the sole plate of the partition wall. We used a level to transfer the location of the end of the tub to the floor. Then we removed the tub and attached the sole plate with deck screws.

How to install an alcove bathtub (cont.)

9 Build a 2 × 4 partition wall if you're creating an alcove for the new tub. The outer stud in the wall should be flush with the tub apron. Nail or screw the sole plate to the subfloor so it will be aligned with the foot of the tub. Use a level bound to a straight 2 × 4 to transfer the location of the sole plate onto the ceiling so you can position a cap plate that's aligned with it. Attach the cap plate at ceiling joist locations, then nail the end studs and filler stud into position.

Partition wall sole plate ←

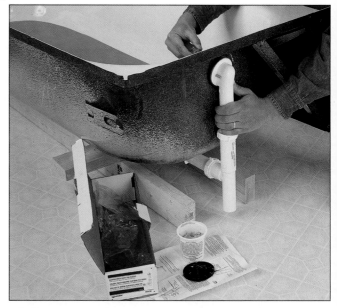

10 Before installing the tub, assemble and attach the drain-waste-overflow kit. The drain flange should be set into a bed of plumber's putty (See step 2, page 121) and the pop-up drain (if your kit has one) should be connected from the drain tailpiece to the overflow coverplate with an adjustable lift rod.

TIP: To reduce noise and conserve heat, wrap the tub with unfaced fiberglass insulation batting before installation. Secure the batting with string or binder's twine.

11 Bathtubs (except claw-foot tubs) should be set into a thin mortar bed to prevent them from moving when they're filled with water, which can cause plumbing seals to fail. Trowel a layer of thinset mortar about ½ in. thick into the tub area using a square-notched trowel. The mortar also allows you to level the tub more accurately.

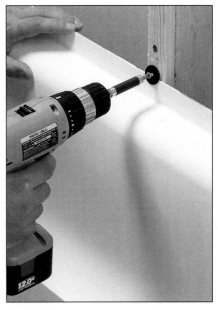

12 Lay a couple of 2 × 4s over the mortar bed to function as glides so you can slip the tub into position without disturbing the mortar. Rest the ends of the 2 × 4s on the sole plate of the wall. Slide the tub into place then remove the glides. Climb into the tub (with surface protector in place) so the rim rests firmly on the wall cleat. NOTE: Make sure the slip nut is threaded onto the drain tailpiece before installing the tub, and double-check to make sure the tailpiece is centered over the drain opening.

13 While standing in the tub, drive 1¼ in. screws with washers into the wall studs above the flange. The washers should overlap the flange, pinning it in place. Don't screw through the flange. Allow the mortar bed to cure.

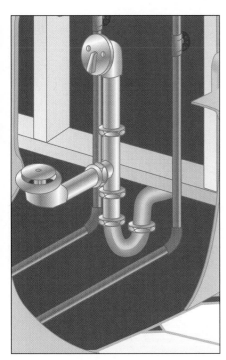

14 Connect the tailpiece of the drain-waste-overflow assembly to the drain trap. Work through the access panel on the opposite side of the plumbing wall to make the connections. Don't over-tighten the slip nut on the drain tailpiece.

15 Attach strips of metal flashing around the perimeter of the tub, leaving a gap of about ¼ in. between the bottom of the flashing strips and the tub rim. This simply provides additional insurance against water penetration into the wall. Apply caulk between the tub apron and the floor. If you're installing a tileboard tub surround kit, patch the walls and cover the partition wall with greenboard (water-resistant wallboard) then install the kit following the manufacturer's instructions. To install a ceramic tile surround, continue on to page 128.

Tips for tiling

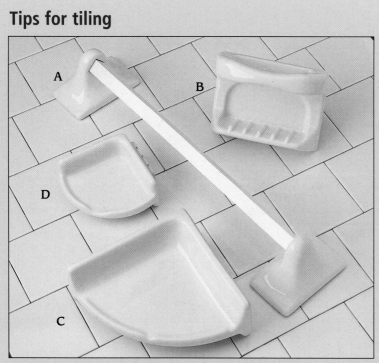

Mortared-in-place accessories for tile tub surrounds include: towel rod (A); soap dish (B); large corner shelf (C); and small corner shelf (D).

Tape cementboard seams with fiberglass mesh tape to form a continuous subbase for the tile. Thinset mortar can be used as the "joint compound" for cementboard. See the section on "Installing tile countertops" (pages 96 to 102) for more information on ceramic tile.

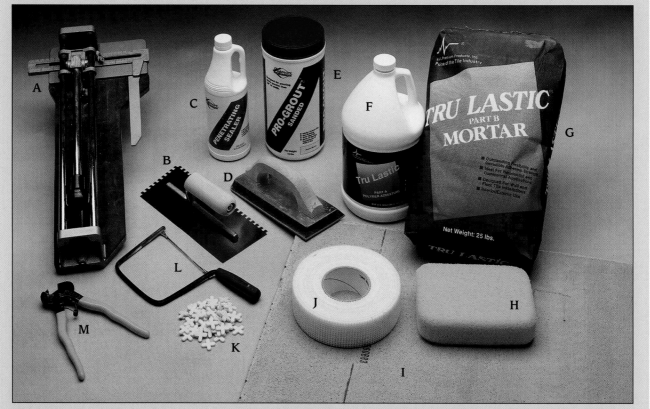

Tools and materials for installing ceramic tile include: Tile cutter (A); notched trowel (B); grout sealer (C); grout float (D); sanded or unsanded grout depending on joint width (E); latex grout additive (F); thinset mortar (G); grout sponge (H); cementboard (I); fiberglass seam tape (J); tile spacers (K); and rod saw (L) or tile nippers (M) for making cutouts in tiles.

How to install a tile tub surround

1 Install the bathtub (See previous pages), then begin the tile tub surround installation by stapling a moisture barrier to the stud walls in the alcove. We stapled strips of 15# building paper to the wall studs, starting at the tub flange and working up toward the top. The paper should overlap the tub flange. Overlap courses by at least 6 in., working in rows from the tub up toward the ceiling. Mark the stud locations on the tub with tape to aid in locating screws when attaching cementboard.

2 Install tile backer board. While some building codes may allow you to use wallboard with a water-resistant covering (greenboard) a better material choice is cementboard. Only the outer skin of the greenboard is moisture-resistant, whereas cementboard will not decay or disintegrate if directly exposed to moisture. We did use greenboard to patch walls around the tile area and to cover the untiled portions of the partition wall. Leave a ¼ in. gap between the backer board and the tub curb.

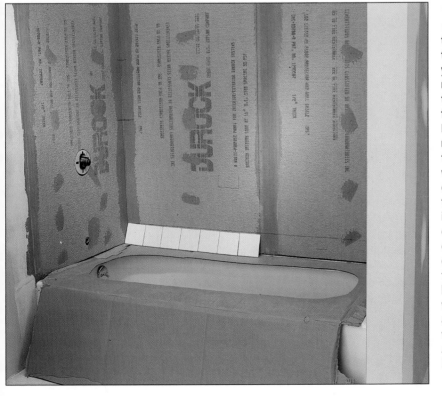

3 Draw layout lines for the tiles. It takes a bit of trial-and-error to arrive at a layout that looks balanced and requires minimal cutting of tiles. Start by checking to make sure your tub is level. If it is, draw a horizontal reference on each wall, measuring up from the tub curb the height of one tile, plus ⅛ in. for an expansion gap under the first course. Measure in several spots then connect the marks to create the line. Also mark the top of the layout area on your wall for reference when applying tile adhesive. Make a dry run of tiles, standing them on end and leaning them against each wall. Start with a full tile in one corner and work toward the opposite end. If the last tile in the dry run is at least one-half tile wide (after cutting) the layout doesn't need adjustment. But if the tile is less than one-half width, shift the tiles so you'll be starting and ending with cut tiles of equal width. Once you have established this arrangement, draw a vertical reference mid-way along the wall at a gap between tiles. Also outline mortared-in-place accessories like soap dishes (See page 128).

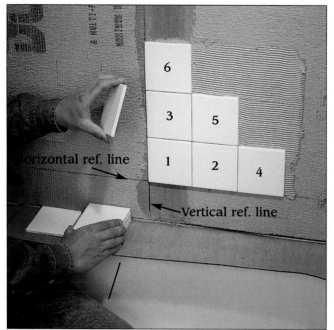

4 Begin tiling on the back wall, at the intersection of the horizontal reference line and the vertical reference line drawn near the midpoint of the wall. Apply a layer of latex-fortified thinset mortar to the wall, using the trowel specified by the adhesive manufacturer (a ³⁄₁₆ in. V-notch trowel was used above). Before setting the first tiles, slip a ⅛ in. thick spacer on the tub curb. Set the first tile in place, pushing it into the mortar bed with a slight twisting motion. Install the next five tiles in the order indicated above. Most wall tile sold today is fashioned with integral spacing lugs to set distances automatically. If your tiles don't have built-in lugs, use plastic tile spacers.

5 Continue adding tiles, building up and out toward the end walls in a pyramid on each side of the vertical reference line. When you reach mortared-in-place accessories, install them as if they were regular tiles, cutting adjoining field tiles as needed to fit around the accessories in the area you outlined. Secure the accessories with masking tape until the mortar cures. When you reach the end walls, be sure the tiles are no closer than ⅛ in. to the wall (you may even want to use spacers here).

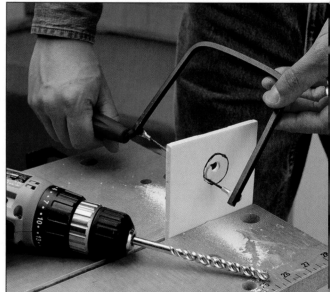

6 Complete the back wall. The top row of tiles should be bullnose tiles. Then repeat the process to tile the end walls at the foot and head of the tub. Do the foot wall first since it's usually a little easier. In our case, we designed the partition wall to accommodate a full row of bullnose tiles stacked vertically next to the tub. The cut tile was positioned at the bottom.

7 Tile the head wall. Because this wall typically contains several obstacles, it is the trickiest wall to tile. You'll need to cut tiles to fit around the shower arm pipe (in most cases), the faucet handle opening, and additional soap dish or corner accessories. Use a rod saw to cut curved shapes as needed into the tiles. For internal cuts, drill an access hole first with a ceramic tile bit. Finish laying tiles at this wall

8 After the mortar has cured (See manufacturer's instructions), mix tile grout (add latex fortifier if it's not included in the grout mix you purchase). Then apply grout to the wall surfaces with the grout float.

9 After the grout has set up slightly, wipe off any remaining grout from the surface with a damp sponge. Run the sponge diagonal to the grout lines, taking care not to draw grout up from the joints. After the grout dries, buff the thin, hazy residue off the tiles using a soft cloth.

10 Let the tiles cure for at least a week before using the shower. Before you use the shower,, caulk the seam between the tiles and the tub curb with silicone bathtub caulk. Also caulk around accessories and plumbing fittings as directed by the manufacturer. Lay a bead of caulk between the tub apron and the floor, if this has not already been done. Finally, apply grout sealer to the grout lines (See step 14, page 102). Then install a shower curtain rod or door (See next page).

How to install a sliding bypass door for a tub surround

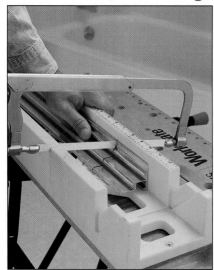

1 Sliding bypass doors consist of two framed door panels made from tempered safety glass or plastic. The panels slide in tracks mounted to the tub curb below and between the walls above the panels. Bypass door kits can be adjusted to fit tub surrounds that are within a standard tub-length range. Measure the width of the surround opening and cut the bottom track to that length minus the combined thickness of the wall jambs (1½ in. as shown above), using a hack saw. Deburr the cut end with emery cloth.

2 Position the bottom track on the tub curb, leaving a recess of about ½ in. between the track and the tub apron. Make sure the recess is the same all along the track, and locate the track so the spaces between the ends and the walls are the same (¾ in. as shown). Secure the track with masking tape. Then, set the jambs in place so they're aligned properly with the bottom track (See manufacturer's instructions). Use a level to make sure the jambs are exactly vertical, then secure the jambs and mark drilling points for screw holes at the predrilled guide holes in the jambs.

3 Before removing the track and jambs, lightly mark their positions with a pencil. Then, remove the parts. Attach the bottom track by applying silicone caulk to the surfaces that contact the tub, and pressing it in place (do not use screws or other metal fasteners). Attach the jambs with the fasteners provided by the manufacturer (usually screws and rubber "bumper" type washers). Then, cut the top frame to size and fit it over the jambs.

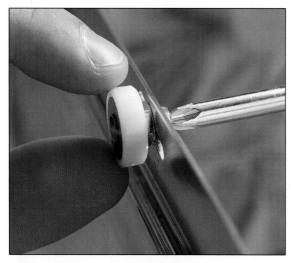

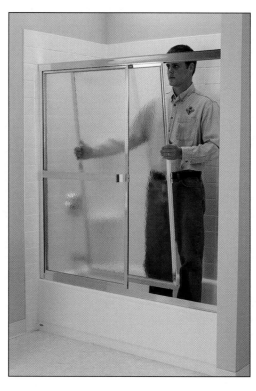

4 Attach rollers, pins and other hardware to the door panels as required by the manufacturer. Make sure you're attaching the correct hardware to each panel (typically, the frame flanges are sized differently on the front and back panels).

5 Set the front glass panel into the forward groove on the bottom track (you'll need to slip it into the top track first, then lower it into the bottom track). Check roller alignment and adjust as directed. Install guide pins to keep the door positioned so it slides smoothly. Then install the back panel in the same manner. Attach any towel bars or handles as necessary, then caulk around the edges of the jambs and tracks, and at joints between tracks and jambs.

Most of the parts of a shower drain kit are assembled and attached to the base prior to installation, then simply locked in place over the drain pipe once the base is installed.

Installing shower stall kits

Shower bases (pans) sold today are almost always sold as kits that generally include parts for attaching the base to your drain pipe, as well as walls for a shower surround. The specific installation steps vary by manufacturer, especially where making the drain hookup is concerned. Generally, the parts of the drain kit are partially assembled and attached to the base then set over the drain pipe and locked into place. The illustration to the left shows an exploded view of the drain kit's parts on the base unit we installed. It is fairly typical of kits.

Prepare for the new stall by removing the old unit and making sure the drain and supply plumbing are in good repair and positioned correctly (some stalls come with supply holes precut into the walls, but many are left uncut so you can position the holes as needed to fit your supply pipes). Most prefabricated shower stalls require that the walls and floor in the installation area be smooth and clean. Scrape off old residue and apply a coat or two or oil-based primer to the stall area. If the wallcovering extends all the way down to the floor, trim it back in the stall area, so the base can be snugged up against the wall studs.

How to install a shower base & stall kit

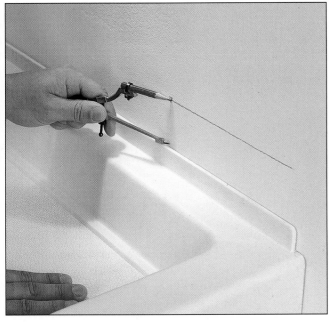

1 When installing a shower base in an area with finished walls (as opposed to new construction with no wall coverings installed), you'll need to cut away the wallcovering around the base so it can be attached directly to the studs. In most cases, make the cutting line about 3 in. above the top flange to create some wiggle room for fitting the base and drain kit assembly over the drain. Use a compass to scribe the profile of the curb onto the wall, then score along the line and pry off the wallcovering with a flat pry bar.

2 With the drain opening clear, set the base into the installation area and check it for level. In many case, you'll need to shim to bring the base to level (unless your unit is set into a bed of thinset mortar, as many are). TIP: Here's a surefire hint for testing the base for level: press a ¼ in. thick ring of plumber's putty around the drain opening to create a dam, then dump a couple of cups of water into the base. When the base is level, the water will form a concentric puddle around the opening, with no random pooling. To shim, use thin strips of exterior plywood or treated lumber (the strips should support the entire side of the base being shimmed).

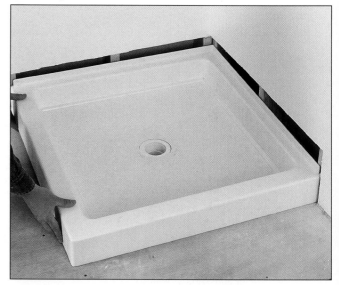

3 Assemble the parts of the drain kit according to the manufacturer's directions and attach it to the base (usually by tightening a lock nut on the under side of the base). Do not attach more parts than are recommended by the manufacturer. Most kits have a locking mechanism that is driven or twisted on the kit from above to fasten it to the drain pipe after the base is positioned and connected.

4 Lubricate the seal portion of the drain kit (the part that fits directly onto the drain pipe) according to the manufacturer's directions (warm, soapy water is a common lubricant). Make sure the lock nut on the underside of the base is fully tightened (but not overtightened), then position the base over the drain pipe. Set the base onto the pipe so the seal fits over the pipe.

5 Lock the base into position. On the model we installed, this is done by driving a retainer wedge into the drain opening. This must be done with some care, as driving too hard can cause cracks or distension of the drain kit. After the fastener is secured (in our case, fully seated against the top of the drain pipe), attach the strainer to the drain assembly. If your shower base is set into mortar, let the mortar cure overnight before proceeding with the installation. NOTE: Some manufacturers recommend that you attach the flanges of the base to wall studs with either screws or nails. Unless it is specifically required, avoid doing this.

6 Mark layout lines on the wall for the surround panels, according to the manufacturer's directions. For the surround we installed, we marked vertical lines 30½ in. out from each corner and a level top line 68 in. up from the top of the base curb. Then, position the panels against the lines and tape them together temporarily with masking tape. Make sure that all overlaps between panels are within the range specified by the manufacturer (at least ½ in., but not more than 1 in., for the model shown here). If overlap exceeds the maximum, mark the panel that is overlapped and trim it to size by scoring with a sharp utility knife and snapping.

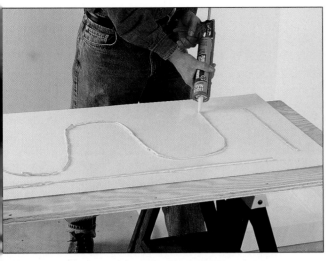

7 Attach the wall panel that doesn't contain cutouts for plumbing connections. Apply beads of panel adhesive formulated for bathroom panel installations to the back of the panel. The beads should be about ¼ in. in diameter and applied in a continuous "S" shape in the center of the panel. Apply straight lines of adhesive about 2 in. in from each edge. Press the panel into position, making sure to keep the bottom edge flush against the curb. Wrap a short piece of 2 × 4 with an old towel or cloth and use it to rub the panel to set it into the adhesive.

8 Mark cutouts on the wall panel that will fit over the plumbing stubouts. If the cardboard shipping carton for the surround is in good repair, use it as a template for locating the holes. Cut the shower arm hole with a hole saw sized no more than ¼ in. larger than the diameter of the pipe. Use a utility knife to cut for the faucet assembly. Attach the panel, taking care to get a good seal with the first panel. If your surround has a corner panel, as ours does, install it after the plumbing wall panel. For alcove installations, install the third wall panel.

9 For corner units with no partition wall, install the support structure for the exposed shower wall (usually a clear, fixed panel). The kit we installed employs a system of U-shaped jambs that mount to the walls, and a frame network that supports the fixed panels from above and below. Finish installation of frame.

10 Complete the installation by hanging the shower door or doors. In the model shown here, a pair of narrow doors fit together in the front corner and slide apart next to the fixed panels to allow access to the shower. The doors are mounted with a system of pins and screws. Hang the doors then caulk the stall unit as directed. Attach shower heads and faucet handles.

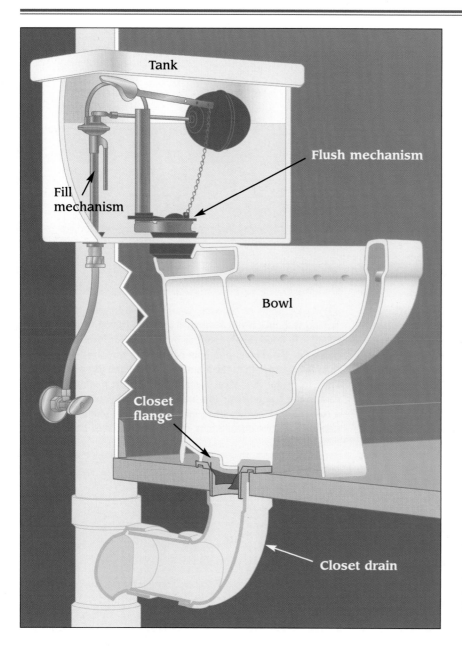

Replacing a toilet

Removing an old toilet that's out of date or in poor repair and replacing it with a new model is not especially difficult or time-consuming, although it can get a little messy at times. Even if your current toilet is working just fine, you may want to consider replacing it with a modern low-flow model, typically using only 1.6 gallons of water per flush (compared to 3 gallons or even more on some older·models). The savings on your water bill may not completely offset the cost of the new unit, but it's an environmentally responsible act of remodeling. And in many localities, low-flow toilets are now required by building codes.

Before you purchase your new toilet, take some measurements on the old one. Fixtures made before the 1960s were often deeper from front to back than newer models. As a result, the closet drain for the toilet is farther from the wall, leaving you two options: move the drain (a very laborious chore) or learn to live with a 2 in. gap behind the toilet tank. You may be able to find a larger toilet, but perhaps the best solution is to install an offset flange that allows you to move the drain opening back without moving the drain.

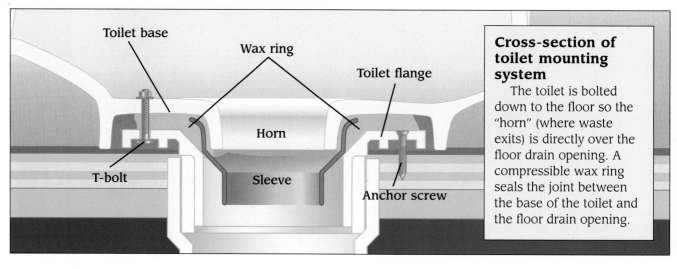

Cross-section of toilet mounting system

The toilet is bolted down to the floor so the "horn" (where waste exits) is directly over the floor drain opening. A compressible wax ring seals the joint between the base of the toilet and the floor drain opening.

Buyers' choice: one-piece or two piece toilets

One-piece toilets have a sleek, low-profile appearance and, because there is no joint between the tank and the bowl, they are less likely to develop leaks. But they are also considerably more expensive.

Two-piece toilets are considerably more common than one-piece models due mostly to their lower cost. They are also easier to transport, and they come in a very wide range of styles and colors.

How to remove a toilet

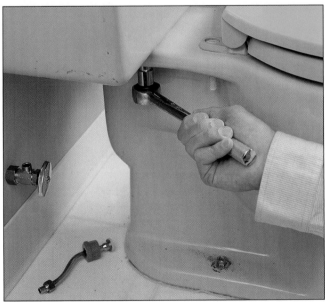

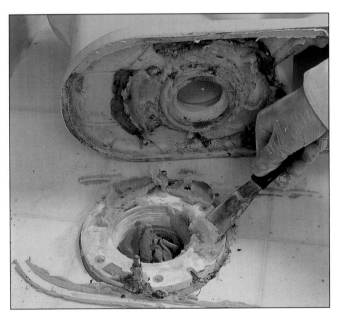

1 Shut off the water supply at the stop valve and empty the tank by flushing the toilet. To remove the tank, first disconnect the water supply tube at the shutoff valve and at the bottom of the tank. Then, use a ratchet wrench to disconnect the the tank bolts that hold the tank to the base. Lift the tank off the bowl and set it aside. Soak up water with a sponge. If you're not reinstalling the toilet, discard the old unit immediately.

2 Remove the trim caps and nuts that anchor the stool to the closet bolts protruding up through the floor. Lift the stool off the wax ring, rocking gently if need be to break the bond. Set the stool aside, then plug the drain opening temporarily with a rag. Inspect the flange to make sure it isn't damaged, then scrape off the wax from the old wax ring.

Options for raising a low toilet flange

Replacing a floorcovering often results in a floor surface that's higher than the top of the toilet flange. There are several ways to correct this problem. An extra-thick wax ring can be used to fill the void (left photo); a simple PVC spacer can be fitted over the top of the flange; or a waxless flange spacer assembly can be installed (right photo).

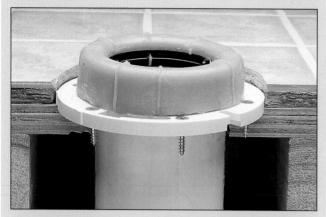

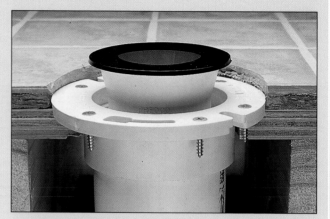

Use an extra-thick wax ring if the top of the current flange is level with or slightly below the surface of the floor that will contact the toilet base. This is a better method than stacking two standard wax rings together (a common practice that's not recommended).

A waxless flange spacer ring can be installed on top of the original flange to form a seal around the toilet horn. Consisting of a plastic ring and flexible rubber gasket, a spacer ring assembly is a neater solution than a wax ring.

How to install a toilet

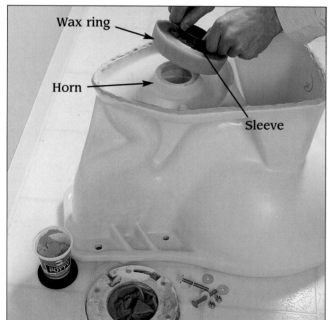

Wax ring

Horn

Sleeve

1 Make sure the old wax ring is cleaned completely from the toilet flange. Replace or augment the flange if needed (See Options, above). With the stool resting upside-down, slip a wax ring gasket around the horn of the toilet and press it lightly against the base. Roll a "snake" from plumber's putty and apply it around the bottom of the stool to form a seal where it contacts the floor.

2 Insert T-bolts (also called closet or floor bolts) head-first into the wide ends of the slots in the flange, then slide them into the slots until the two bolts form a line parallel to the back wall. To make it easier to align the bolt holes in the stool base with the bolts, slip rigid tubing over the bolts. Carefully lower the stool onto the flange so the bolts fit into the openings in the base (this is a good time to have a helper).

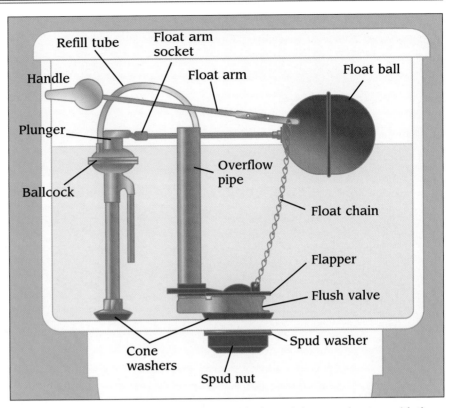

3 Make sure the front of the stool is parallel to the back wall, then press down evenly on the rim to seat the stool in the wax ring and plumber's putty. A board placed over the rim will help distribute pressure more evenly.

4 Install or hook up the flush mechanism inside the tank (some tanks come with the mechanism preinstalled). Thread the spud washer onto the tailpiece of the flush valve NOTE: Flush mechanisms come in several styles, including the ballfloat type (above) and the cup float style. **Follow the manufacturer's directions.**

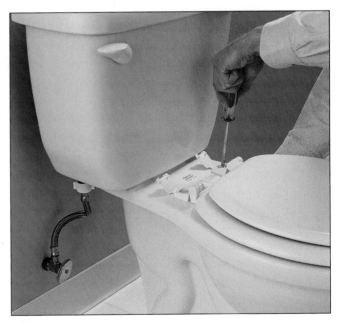

5 Set the tank onto the stool so the spud washer and tailpiece fit into the water inlet opening. The tank bolt holes in the tank and in the stool should be aligned. Slip rubber washers onto the tank bolts, then thread them through the holes in the bottom of the tank and secure them with washers and nuts. Be careful not to overtighten the nuts.

6 Attach a new supply tube to the shutoff valve, then attach the other end to the tailpiece for the fill valve that protrudes through the bottom of the tank. Use plumber's putty to seal the connection. Open the shutoff valve and check for leaks. Attach the toilet seat and the trim caps for the floor bolts.

Lighting, Wiring & Ventilation

Into just about any kitchen or bathroom remodeling project, a little wiring work must fall. New lights need to be hooked up. Old duplex receptacles need to be replaced with ground fault circuit interrupter receptacles. Ventilation may need to be installed. Or you may need to add entirely new wiring circuits to bring your house up to code and to make it more livable. In all these cases, you can save a tremendous amount of money by doing all or most of the work yourself.

More than most DIY projects, working with wiring, lighting and ventilation are tasks that appeal to the thinking handyman. They require research, both in the field (where is that circuit coming from?) and in the den or the library (how many cubic feet of air per minute should my new bath fan move?). And while some may find these challenges a little intimidating, if not outright boring, learning electrical systems and developing your home wiring skills are both excellent investments of time.

In this chapter we have included some basic information about wiring, along with specific information about how to conduct a number of popular do-it-yourself projects. As you apply the information you learn and the plans you've made, remember to never take any electrical project for granted. Always use extreme caution, and do not make the mistake of overstepping the limits of your knowledge and experience.

Undercabinet lights are easy to install and they project light directly onto your kitchen work areas, where it's needed most.

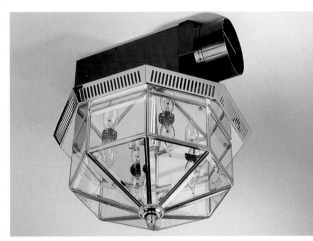

Vent fans don't have to be boring. For kitchens or for baths ,you can find a vent fan that's both attractive and hardworking.

Electrical Codes

The information found on these pages conforms to the National Electrical Code requirements. These requirements ensure safe, durable wiring installations that will best serve your needs. But your wiring project may have additional requirements not covered by the Code. Also, the Code requirements in your community may differ from those in the National Code. Local Code always takes precedence in these situations. Always check with your local electrical inspector to make certain your project will comply with local standards. If your wiring project is part of a larger remodeling or building project that includes plumbing work, remember that plumbing has the right-of-way. Always do the plumbing installation before beginning any wiring work in that area.

Ceiling lights come in an array of shapes, sizes and styles. The contemporary pendant light above can serve as a feature light in the center of the ceiling, or it can be placed strategically to illuminate a favorite feature, such as a kitchen island.

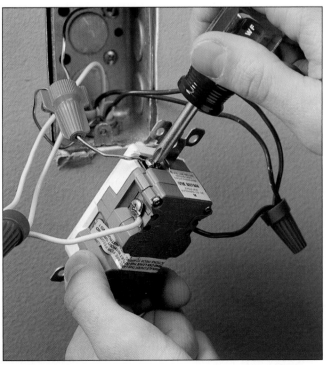

Stay current with electrical code by replacing ordinary outlet receptacles with ground fault circuit interrupter (GFCI) receptacles throughout your kitchen and bathroom.

Some basics of working with wiring

It goes without saying, but bears repeating, that household electrical current is extremely dangerous and should be treated with great caution. If you feel intimidated by the prospect of performing any home-improvement tasks that involve wiring, you are most likely in the majority. After all, a single mistake can have catastrophic consequences. But if you're willing to do a little studying and you're capable of working carefully, you should find the lighting, wiring and ventilation projects shown and discussed in this chapter to be quite manageable.

Household electrical wiring is a little bit like one of those 3D wall puzzles, where if you stare at it long enough all of a sudden a clear image will leap out from the meaningless streaks and blurs of color. There really is a rhyme and reason to how electricity behaves and the way houses are wired. There is not space in this chapter to spend a lot of time dissecting the fundamental properties of electricity. But if you attempt one or two basic wiring projects, you may find that not only do they work, but you enjoyed them and you want to learn more.

The basic information shown on this page and the next should provide you with just enough familiarity with the subject matter that you can follow along and understand the instructions that come with your new ceiling light or vent fan. But anytime you are the least bit unsure of what to do, stop and seek assistance.

Testing for electrical current

 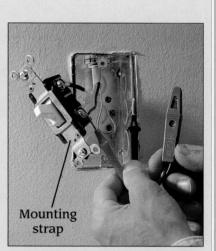

Mounting strap

At a receptacle: Turn off power at the main panel. Insert the circuit tester probes into the receptacle slots. Check both halves of the receptacle. If the tester glows, power is still present. Turn off the appropriate circuit and test again. Also see page 149, Step 1.

At a switch: Turn off power at the main panel. Carefully pull the switch out of the box, touching only the mounting strap. Touch one circuit tester probe to the grounded metal box or bare copper grounding wire. Touch the other probe to each screw terminal. If the tester glows, power is present.

Pigtails connect multiple wires to a single screw terminal

A *pigtail* is used to connect two or more wires to one screw terminal, since only one wire may be attached to a terminal. Cut a short length of wire of the same color as the wires that need connecting. (Keep excess cable pieces for this purpose.) Strip ½ in. of insulation off of one end, then strip ¾ in. off the other end and make a hook. Attach the hook end to the terminal, then connect the other end to the wires.

Use a wire connector when connecting wires together. Strip ½ in. of sheathing from the end of each wire. Hold the wires so the stripped ends are parallel, with their ends aligned. Place the wire connector over the wire ends and twist it onto the ends in a clockwise direction. Continue turning the connector until the sheathed portions of the wires begin to twist together. The photo at right illustrates how

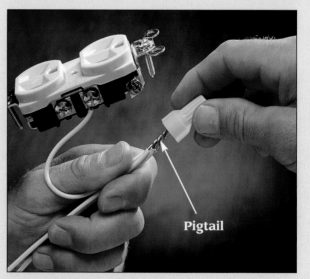

Pigtail

the wire connector twists the bare ends of the individual wires tightly together. No bare wire should extend past the bottom of the connector.

How to strip NM (nonmetallic) cable with cable rippers

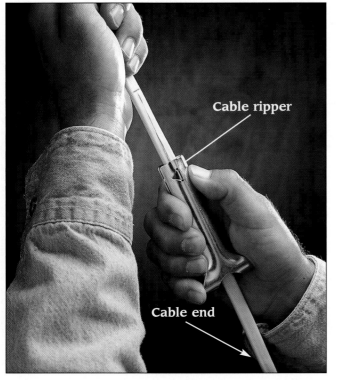

1 Use a cable ripper to cut through the cable sheathing without damaging the wires inside. This works best on cable containing two wires with ground. Insert the cable through the ripper, then firmly press the arms together, forcing the cutting tip into the sheathing. Pull the ripper to the end of the cable to cut through the sheathing.

2 After cutting through the cable sheathing, peel the sheathing and the paper wrapper back, then cut them off with a utility knife or wire cutters. Be careful that you don't nick the wire insulation as you perform this operation.

Preparing wires for making connections

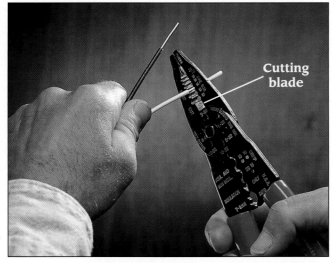

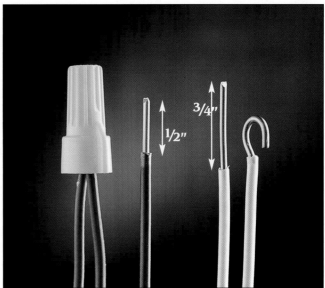

Use a combination wire stripping tool to cut individual wires to length and to strip off the insulation. After using the tool's cutting blade to cut a wire to correct length, open the combination tool jaws and place the end of the wire into the opening in the tool that matches the wire gauge. Close the jaws and pull the tool to the end of the wire to remove the insulation. Take care to avoid nicking the wire.

When stripping individual wires, remove ½ in. of insulation if using a wire connector (left) or ¾ in. of insulation when you will make a hook to attach to a screw terminal (right). No bare wire should show beyond the bottom of the wire connector, and insulation should end at the screw terminal.

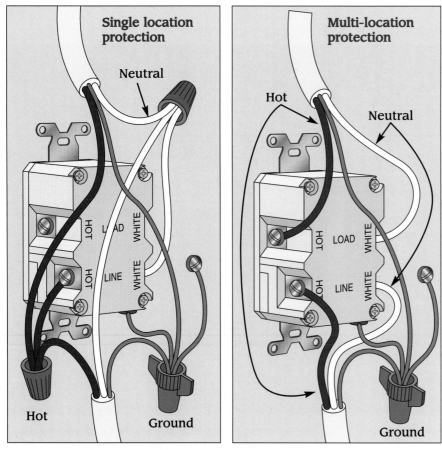

There are basically two ways to wire a GFCI outlet: for a single location or for multiple locations. With the single location method, only the receptacle itself is protected from electric shock. In multi-location wiring configurations, the GFCI receptacle will also sense irregular electrical flow at any point in the circuit further down the line.

Installing a GFCI receptacle

Ground fault circuit interrupters (GFCI's) aren't just a good idea: They're the law. GFCI-protected receptacles have sensors that cause them to shut down instantly if they detect a sudden, significant change in the flow of electrical current. If it's plugged into a GFCI outlet, an appliance that short circuits won't cause electrical damage or fire. And because the possibility of a short circuit is much higher in damp areas, these safety devices are now required by the Uniform Building Code at every bathroom and kitchen receptacle.

In private residences, the GFCI requirement is enforced only on new construction and on remodeling projects where an electrical permit is pulled. Nevertheless, if you're kitchen or bathroom is not equipped with them, it's worth a few dollars and a couple of hours to make the switch.

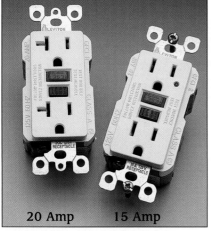

Choose a GFCI receptacle with the correct amperage rating for your location. In kitchens or bathrooms with a series of protected receptacles, it's generally accepted practice to use 15-amp receptacles on 20-amp circuits (receptacles are rated *20-in, 15-out*). Dedicated 20-amp circuits, as may be required for microwaves or refrigerator/freezers, should have a 20-amp GFCI receptacle.

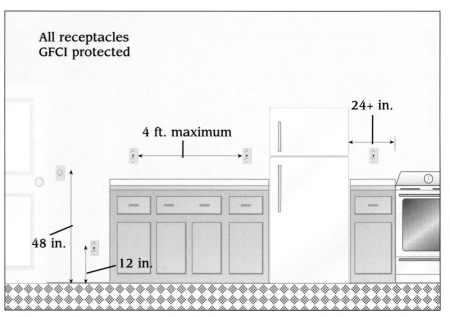

Uniform Electrical Code requires that all electrical receptacles in kitchens and bathrooms be GFCI-protected, regardless of its proximity to a water source. The Code also mandates that kitchens be well served with separate electrical circuits for small appliances, electric ovens, dishwashers and disposers. There must be at least one receptacle along every four feet of wall space.

How to replace a duplex receptacle with a single location GFCI receptacle

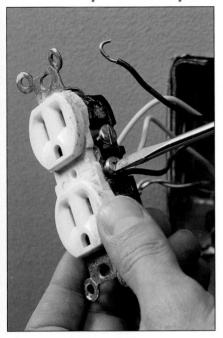

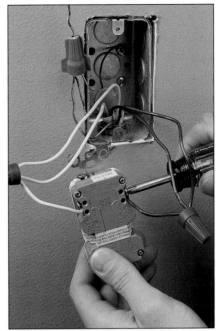

1 At the main service panel, shut off power to the circuit by flipping the circuit breaker or removing the fuse. Use a neon circuit tester to make sure power is not flowing into the receptacle (See page 142), then remove the coverplate. Remove the mounting screws, holding the receptacle to the box then withdraw the receptacle. Disconnect the wires at the terminals.

2 Cut 3 to 4 in. long black and white pigtail wires of matching gauge and case color, stripping away about ½ in. of casing from each end of each wire. Gang each pigtail with the LOAD and LINE wire of the same color, using a wire connector of suitable size. Twist the wires together with pliers before adding the connector.

3 Connect the white pigtail wire to the terminal identified as WHITE LINE. Make sure the wire is fully inserted into the slot and tighten the set screw. Test to make sure wire is secure by pulling lightly on it. Connect the black pigtail to the HOT LINE terminal.

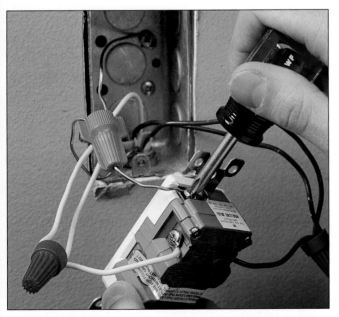

4 Cut two 4 to 6 in. long bare copper ground wires and twist them together, with the bare grounds coming into and exiting the receptacle box. Form a loop on one end of each unconnected wire. Attach one to the ground screw on the receptacle and the other to the ground screw on the box.

5 Arrange the wires so they will fit into the box, being careful not to disrupt connections. Tuck the wires into the box and attach the GFCI receptacle to the box using the mounting screws. Attach the coverplate, turn the power on, then push the "SET" button on the receptacle. Test with a receptacle tester to make sure wiring is correct.

Lighting basics

Well-chosen and well-placed lighting fixtures make a room more pleasant, safer and easier to function in. Lighting can also add drama and it can highlight the best features of the room, as in the bar area of the kitchen shown above.

An upgrade in lighting can transform a kitchen or bathroom like few other projects. It could be as simple as adding a strategically placed table lamp or as extravagant as a new bay window to let the natural sunlight pour in. But most frequently, when we think of lighting we concentrate on permanently mounted light fixtures. In this category, options abound and the impact can be immediate and very dramatic.

Planning a lighting scheme is a tricky job. If there is any part of your remodeling project to consult a professional on, believe it or not, this may well be the one. The study of light (how it is reflected, how it is observed, even how it makes us feel) is a complex science and even the most humble kitchen or bathroom could benefit from a bit of rigorous evaluation and some informed opinions. But if you're a true do-it-yourselfer at heart, you're probably plenty willing to take a crack at designing a lighting scheme. Well, here's a good place for anyone to start: Invest in a ceiling fixture that sheds plenty of light (but equip it with a dimmer switch) and appeals to you visually. Then, decide which parts of the room you use the most and throw a light on each of them (See below for ideas).

Light sources

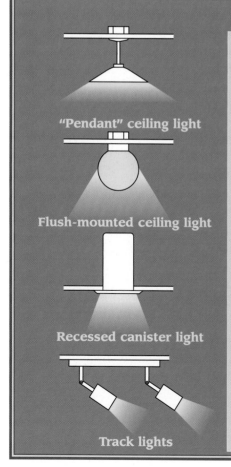

"Pendant" ceiling light

Flush-mounted ceiling light

Recessed canister light

Track lights

For variety and efficiency, kitchens and bathrooms normally have multiple light sources. The basic types of light are:

Direct overhead light. A prominent ceiling fixture creates a base of light for either room that may not be romantic or moody, but is very important. The fixture itself is often a design focal point in the room. Overhead light can be incandescent or fluorescent, and flush-mounted or suspended, as with pendant lights or chandeliers.

Task lighting. Recessed canister lights or track lights with reflective, incandescent bulbs are the norm. They provide intense, warm light that's directed to a specific area, such as cooktop or shower.

Undercabinet light. Usually fluorescent or halogen, undercabinet lights spread a diffuse glow onto countertop areas that would otherwise be in constant shadow.

Indirect light. Lights, usually fluorescent, mounted to wall cabinets and bounced off a light colored ceiling for a light that appears sourceless.

Wall lights. Sconces are installed mostly for decoration or to create a romantic mood. Mirror lights frame a vanity mirror at the sides and/or top.

Natural light. Nothing compares to it. Bring in as much as you can.

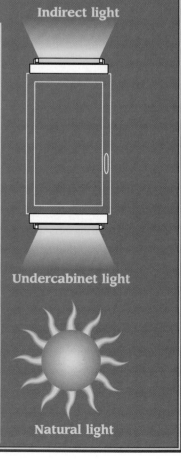

Indirect light

Undercabinet light

Natural light

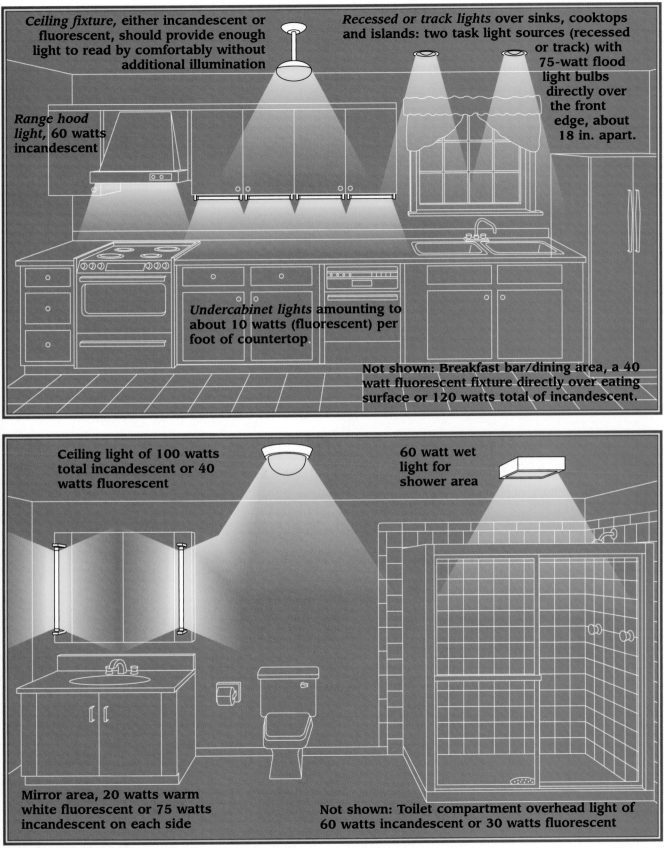

Ceiling fixture, either incandescent or fluorescent, should provide enough light to read by comfortably without additional illumination

Recessed or track lights over sinks, cooktops and islands: two task light sources (recessed or track) with 75-watt flood light bulbs directly over the front edge, about 18 in. apart.

Range hood light, 60 watts incandescent

Undercabinet lights amounting to about 10 watts (fluorescent) per foot of countertop.

Not shown: Breakfast bar/dining area, a 40 watt fluorescent fixture directly over eating surface or 120 watts total of incandescent.

Ceiling light of 100 watts total incandescent or 40 watts fluorescent

60 watt wet light for shower area

Mirror area, 20 watts warm white fluorescent or 75 watts incandescent on each side

Not shown: Toilet compartment overhead light of 60 watts incandescent or 30 watts fluorescent

There are many ways to measure "adequate" lighting, from very scientific (ranging from 20 to 200 footcandles depending on the difficulty of the task you're performing), to common sense: "You can never have too much light." But here are some general guidelines for ideal lighting that may prove of use when updating a kitchen or bathroom.

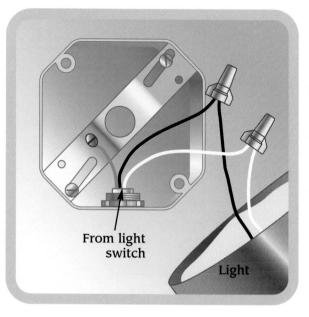

From light switch

Light

Situation 1: One cable entering the light fixture box indicates that the light fixture alone is controlled by the light switch. This is a relatively easy wiring situation: simply unhook the old wires then connect black to black and white to white and ground the bare copper.

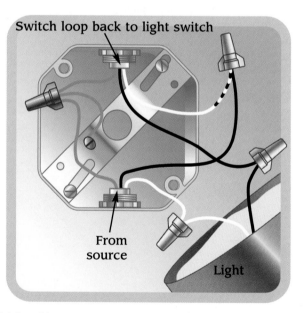

Switch loop back to light switch

From source

Light

Multiple cables entering the light fixture box means that the current bypasses the fixture when it enters the box and heads directly to the switch via the tagged white wire (black tape on a white wire indicates that it is hot, not neutral). If the switch is turned on, the current goes through the switch and returns back to the light fixture via the black wire. In this situation, connect the black wire from the new light fixture to the black wire that's paired with the tagged white wire (called a switch loop). The black (hot) lead from the power source is connected to the tagged wire, and the white neutral from the source is connected to the white wire on the fixture.

New

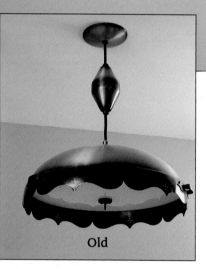

Even the simple walls of this plain room seemed somehow more elegant and at ease when this old, tacky ceiling light was replaced with a lovely new pendant style fixture.

Old

Ceiling light fixtures

Replacing an out of date or underpowered ceiling light can be accomplished in just a few minutes (or, naturally, it can also take longer). In the perfect remove-and-replace situation, the old fixture would have been installed correctly, with clean, visible connections. The light fixture box would be securely mounted in the ceiling, none of the screws would be missing or stripped, and the escutcheon plate for the new light fixture would cover the hole in the ceiling perfectly. For an example of such an installation, see the sequence on the following page. Although your situation may not be quite as text-book, you'll find that the basic steps are pretty much the same.

How to replace a ceiling light

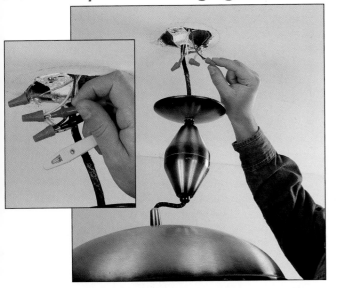

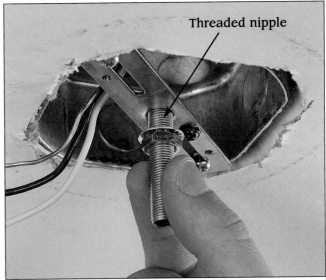

Threaded nipple

1 Shut off power to the electrical circuit at the main service panel. Remove diffusers, shades and bulbs to provide access to the coverplate of the light fixture. Remove the coverplate (either by removing mounting screws or loosening the retaining nut that's attached to a threaded nipple that projects from the mounting strap on the electrical box in the ceiling). Gently draw the fixture away from the box to expose the wire connectors. Insert the probes of a neon circuit tester into the wire connector to make sure power is off (inset photo).

2 Disconnect the wires and ground (if any—older homes may not have one). If supply wires are not color coded, label the hot lead by wrapping it with a small piece of electrical tape. Attach the mounting strap provided with your new light to the electrical box using the box mounting screws. Make sure the existing box is large enough to house the new light fixture wiring (See manufacturer's directions). Also attach the threaded nipple into the threaded hole in the mounting bracket.

3 Assemble the new fixture as required. Most light fixtures, especially more complex units intended for the kitchen, require a significant amount of assembly and wire threading before they can be hooked up. Assemble the new unit as completely as you can (it's much easier to do this now than after it's partially hanging from the ceiling) but don't install globes, diffusers or bulbs yet.

4 With a helper supporting heavier fixtures, thread the fixture wires up through the tube in the mounting strap then secure the lock washer or retaining nut that secures the fixture to the ceiling. Adjust any chains or cables as directed to set the height of pendant-style fixtures, then trim wires back so 6 to 8 in. is free in the electrical box. Strip insulation at the ends to expose ½ in. of bare wire, then make hot, neutral and ground connections with a wire connector as directed. Attach coverplate to electrical box, then secure the escutcheon plate. Install bulbs and diffusers. Turn power on and test.

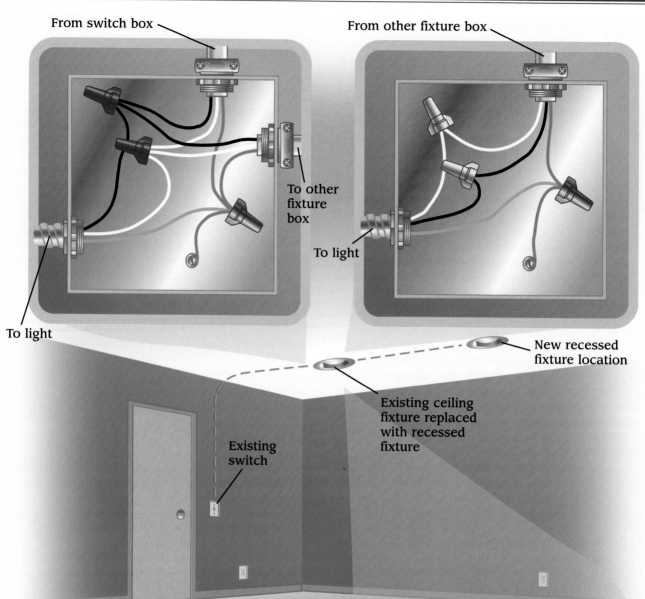

From switch box

From other fixture box

To other fixture box

To light

To light

To light

New recessed fixture location

Existing ceiling fixture replaced with recessed fixture

Existing switch

Recessed lights

Replacing an existing ceiling fixture with a recessed light fixture is relatively easy. You can add additional recessed fixtures at the same time. These wiring diagrams show the self-contained electrical boxes found on recessed fixtures. The armored cable connects the electrical box to the light.

Either one or two cables are connected to the existing ceiling fixture. If there is one cable, power is routed to the switch box first. The diagram above, left shows wire connections for replacing the fixture with a recessed light while adding another recessed light.

If there are two cables, power is routed to the fixture box before going to the switch. The diagram at right shows wire connections for this, again adding another recessed light.

The diagram above, right, shows wire connections for the additional recessed fixture in either situation.

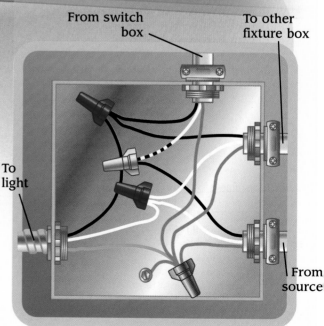

From switch box

To other fixture box

To light

From source

Recessed lights offer warm, directed light, usually provided by a reflective flood light bulb. Because they are so unobtrusive, they don't distract the eye from more interesting sights. They are used mostly for task lighting, but when installed in sufficient number can be used for allover general lighting as well.

Recessed lights

Sometimes called "canister lights," recessed lights aren't designed to contribute significantly to the decor of a room, except to the extent that they shed their light on the objects below them. In kitchens, recessed lights are very frequently installed in soffits that are built out in the area between the tops of the wall cabinets and the ceiling. They can also be stationed over kitchen islands or even in areas where their zero-clearance profile is an advantage (for exam-ple, if you have floor to ceiling cabinets with doors that swing out). In bathrooms, recessed lights are installed in shower areas and sometimes above stalls or over dressing tables. Because of the constant moisture, use special vapor-proof canister lights in these spots. If installing multiple lights, keep in mind that spacing controls the intensity of the light. Generally, recessed lights are installed at intervals between 18 and 36 inches.

How to install a recessed light canister

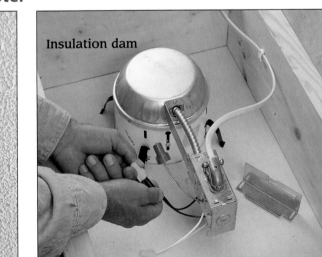

Insulation dam

1 With the power off, run electrical cable (14/2 NM in most cases, unless the cord is in an open attic, in which case you'll need to use armored cable—check local codes) from the switch box to the light location. Make a cutout for the canister, using the template that came with the light fixture. Make sure the hole area is not obstructed by a joist or other wiring then make the cutout with a wallboard saw or hole saw. Slip the fixture unit up into the opening.

2 Mount the canister to the ceiling surface with tension clips. If the ceiling is insulated, attach a dam board several inches away from the canister on each side (this eliminates insulation contact, which can cause the canister to overheat). Make the electrical connections according to the directions. Test the circuit to make sure the light works. From below, install the trim kit and the lens (if any).

Undercabinet lights

The first decision to make if you're considering installing undercabinet lights is whether you want to hard-wire them or plug them into existing receptacles. Hard-wired lights are more reliable, less visible and they don't consume valuable plug-in space. But plug-in lights are much easier to install and you can even move them to a different spot if you change the way you organize your countertops. If your wall cabinets have face frames, low-profile undercabinet light fixtures will be nearly invisible. If not, you can make and attach simple wood valances to conceal them.

Undercabinet lighting can be used to highlight an interesting or decorative countertop, like this countertop and backsplash made of solid surfacing material.

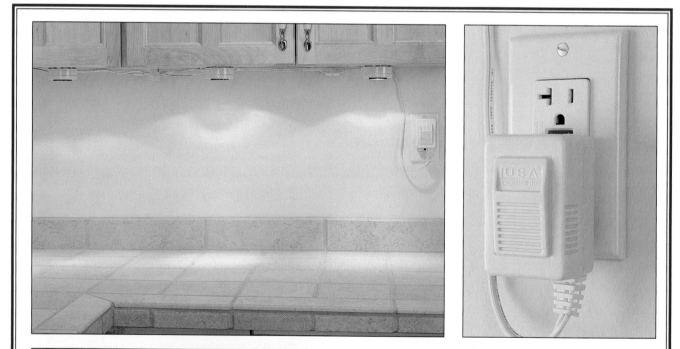

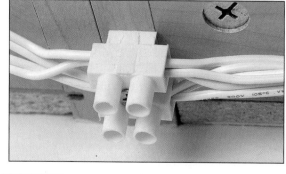

Low voltage halogen lights

These sleek undercabinet lights are barely visible even under frameless cabinets. Installed in series, they cast appealing shafts of soft light onto the countertop, merging together to provide even light below. The 12-volt transformer (above, right) plugs into a wall outlet. It feeds energy efficient power to the lights through a hub mounted at the back of the cabinet area. The leads from the hub to the individual lights can be stapled neatly to the cabinet. The on/off switch is located on the cord near the transformer.

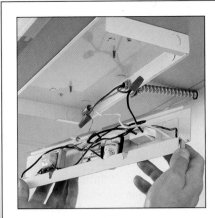

Hard-wired, low-profile fluorescent fixture

With a slim profile of about 1 inch, these slender undercabinet fixtures emit full-power fluorescent light. Because they're hard-wired they have no dangling cords, making them truly unobtrusive. To install them, run armored cable through the wall at the very bottom of the cabinet, then feed the cable into the fixture body. Make connections then snap the bulb-holder into place.

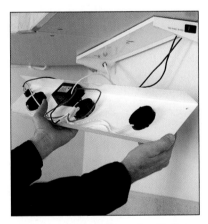

Heavy-duty plug-in light

At 24 in. long, this low-voltage light fixture is built to last, not to hide. An internal transformer reduces power to 20 watts to operate the three halogen lights. It is also easy to mount (just attach the housing to the cabinet then snap the fixture together and plug it in to the nearest outlet).

Kitchen exhaust fans range from simple, very inexpensive wall-mounted range hoods to highly elaborate examples of custom metalwork. The copper fan shown here turns a practical device into a bold design statement.

A somewhat more typical exhaust fan than the towering copper number in the photo above, this stainless steel range hood is well-coordinated with the other steel appliances found in this eclectic kitchen. Many cabinet manufacturers offer range hood covers that match their cabinet styles.

Fans & ventilation

To reduce the amounts of trapped moisture and airborne food and grease particles in your kitchen or bathroom, install a vent fan. In kitchens, the most common vent fan is the familiar range hood. Modest or elaborate, range hoods draw steam, smoke, grease and other air impurities through a filter and vent them out of your house. Removing these particles reduces kitchen maintenance time, keeps the kitchen more comfortable, and really comes in handy when those inevitable small fires flare up. But on the down side, the lower end range hood models tend to make so much noise that we'd rather suffer through a little air pollution than be driven from the kitchen by all the noise pollution. And in the winters, those of us who pay heating bills are given to speculate that "where there's smoke there's warmth" every time we see those clouds of steam rushing up and out of the kitchen.

Range hoods operate on an "updraft" principle, which is great if your oven and stove are against a wall, but not much help if your range top resides in an island or peninsula. For these situations, you can look into a "downdraft" ventilation system. A downdraft unit has horizontal intake vents stationed at the back end of the cooktop. As the name suggests, the downdraft fan draws air down through the cabinet and vents it out of doors—typically through ducts that run between floor joists. Downdraft ventilation systems are generally less effective than updraft models, but many people who own them feel they're better than nothing.

In bathrooms, a bath vent is a near necessity. And many, like the model shown below, have additional features such as lights and even heating elements to make them doubly attractive.

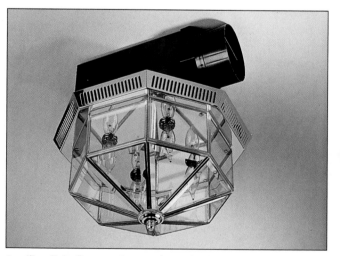

A ceiling light fixture of a popular style cleverly conceals the intake for a bathroom vent fan.

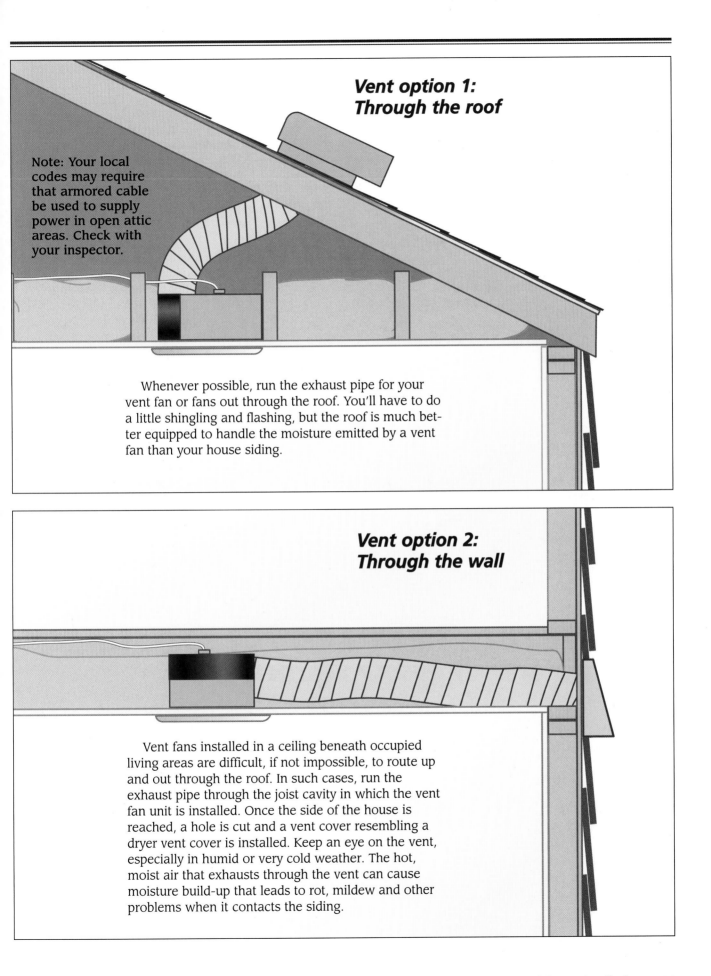

Vent option 1: Through the roof

Note: Your local codes may require that armored cable be used to supply power in open attic areas. Check with your inspector.

Whenever possible, run the exhaust pipe for your vent fan or fans out through the roof. You'll have to do a little shingling and flashing, but the roof is much better equipped to handle the moisture emitted by a vent fan than your house siding.

Vent option 2: Through the wall

Vent fans installed in a ceiling beneath occupied living areas are difficult, if not impossible, to route up and out through the roof. In such cases, run the exhaust pipe through the joist cavity in which the vent fan unit is installed. Once the side of the house is reached, a hole is cut and a vent cover resembling a dryer vent cover is installed. Keep an eye on the vent, especially in humid or very cold weather. The hot, moist air that exhausts through the vent can cause moisture build-up that leads to rot, mildew and other problems when it contacts the siding.

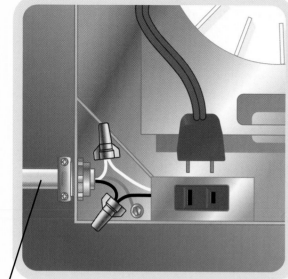

From switch

Bathroom vent fan

You need access to the attic above the bathroom to easily install a vent fan. Purchase a unit containing a light if a switch-controlled ceiling light fixture isn't already present. The illustration at left shows the connections for a fan unit. The diagrams below show connections when the fixture has both a fan and a light. Then the wire connector box on the fan unit would have one more lead, usually red. If ceramic tile covers the walls, it can be difficult to cut a new box opening. The option shown below, right, uses an existing single-gang opening with a double-switch device. However, you can't use a fan timer switch when using this method.

To fan

To fan light

From source

To receptacle

To fan and light

From source

How to install a vent fan box

1 Run electrical service to the vent fan. Fans with heating elements usually require a dedicated circuit. Some municipalities may require that you use armored cable or conduit to run power in exposed areas like attics. From the bathroom, drill a small hole in the ceiling near the center of the planned fan location. Push a length of stiff wire through the hole, into the attic. Locate the wire from the attic, then use the fan box to adjust the position of the opening so the box can be attached to a joist. Cut the opening for the box, then use screws to mount it to the joist.

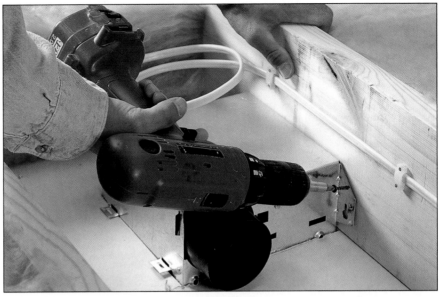

2 Mount the vent cover on the roof or through an exterior side wall and attach the vent hose to the tailpieces on the fan and the vent cover. Remove a knockout on the fan box, then attach cable to the box with a cable clamp. At least ½ in. of sheathing should extend past the cable clamp.

3 Connect the black lead from the fan's wire connection box to the black cable wire; the white lead to the white wire and the cable grounding wire to the grounding clip or screw on the box. Attach the wire connection box to the fan box. Mount the fan motor unit and plug it into the receptacle on the wire connection box. Attach the fan grill. Add an insulation dam if needed (See page 151). Connect flexible vent hose to the box (check your local codes first: some don't allow flexible dryer or vent hose because lint and dust can build up on the flexible ridges, posing a fire hazard) and run it out of the house through a roof or wall (See page 155).

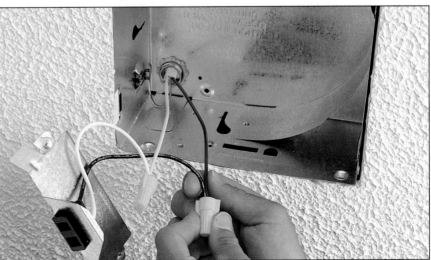

Index